CODING PROJECTS IN FLUTTER

A Hands-On, Project-Based Introduction to Mobile App Development

EDWARD THORNTON

Contents

ONE

Welcome

I wrote this book to broaden my own knowledge of Flutter, and although I still have a way to go, I learned a lot in the process of writing this book. Within these pages, I have tried my best to share all I have learned with you, and I hope you and others who read this book find it all helpful.

Flutter is a simple, high-performance framework based on Dart language. It provides excellent performance for the simple reason that it renders UI directly on Canvas rather than through the native framework. I find it all really fascinating, and I've tried my best to capture what I feel are the essentials of this vast subject in this book. Since it is impossible to condense all there is to Flutter in one book, I've also shared links to websites and resources you can visit for any further information you might need.

In the first half of the book, you'll learn basic programming concepts, such as variables, lists, classes, loops, and algorithms, and you'll be introduced to the Dart language as well as Flutter. You will also learn how to install Flutter and its plugins and how to put your knowledge into practice by developing Flutter projects.

In the second half, you will learn about FlutterFlow, a relatively recent online low-code builder for native mobile apps that run on both iOS and Android. You will also learn how to integrate a FlutterFlow into your projects and how to test your code safely. I will introduce you to Flutter and HTTP, teaching you how to debug safely and all the steps you'll need to take before publishing your app.

As you work through the book, you'll learn how to use powerful Flutter libraries and tools, generate interactive data visualizations, create and customize web apps and deploy them safely online, and how to deal with mistakes and errors so you can solve your own programming problems.

All of these projects have been well thought out, and I have tried to present them in such a way that learning the subject matter and implementing it is an enjoyable pastime, rather than an onerous task to be completed. That being said, I should also point out that despite my best intentions, some of the information in this book may turn out to be incorrect. I tried my best to be as accurate as possible, but the truth is that I still have much to learn about Flutter. Anything wise in these pages you should credit to the many experts who preceded me on this subject. Anything foolish, assume it is my error.

I have also tried to be objective throughout this book, but it is possible that my personal opinions may have shone through in a few pages. Please, if you come across these, try not to take them too seriously. There is no one right way to understand and build with Flutter; this book describes the best way I know.

Happy reading, friend!

TWO

Basic Terminology

A **mobile application (or "mobile app")** is a computer program or software application that runs on a mobile device such as a phone, tablet, or smartwatch. A typical mobile application uses a network connection to work with remote computing resources, and mobile application development is the process of designing software applications that operate on a mobile device. The mobile development process entails building installable software bundles (code, binaries, assets, and so on), integrating backend services like data access through an API, and testing the app on target devices.

Writing mobile apps appears simple, but the sheer amount of platforms available makes it difficult. Your app might run on an iPhone, an iPad, or an Android phone, among other devices. Additionally, these platforms are subject to rapid change as new gadgets enter the market frequently.

Mobile Applications and Device Platforms

In today's market for smart devices, two major platforms reign supreme over all others. These are Apple's iOS platform and Google's Android. The iOS platform is the operating system that runs on Apple's popular iPhone handsets. Many tech companies, alongside Google, use the Android operating system to construct their own smart devices.

While there is some resemblance in terms of app development between the two platforms, designing for iOS vs. designing for Android requires the use of different **software development kits (SDKs)** and development tool chains. Also, Apple utilizes iOS solely for all of its devices, but Google makes Android accessible to most other companies—provided these companies meet certain criteria, such as shipping devices with particular Google applications. Regardless of their differences, modern developers create apps for use on millions of smart devices today leveraging these two platforms.

The goal of this chapter is to provide you with a concise introduction to the world of mobile application development, as well as to get you familiarized with the problem of cross-platform development and how different developers have attempted to tackle it through the years. Before we get started, let's go through some terminology you will encounter over the course of this book.

Compiler

A computer program is a set of instructions that tells the computer how to do something. High-level programming languages are used to create the majority of computer applications. As a result, the computer is unable to comprehend these programs, and they are converted to a machine-readable language. This conversion is carried out by a **compiler**, which is a piece of software that translates the source code into machine code.

An assembler and machine code can be used to create a very rudimentary compiler. You can use the initial compiler to develop a more sophisticated one (then use a second, more refined one to write another, even more sophisticated one) once you have software that can translate language into binary instructions.

A **native compiler** translates a program's source code into machine code for the platform it's running on. The CPU will not need to translate the code in order to interpret and execute it. A **non-native compiler** transforms the source code into a more generic version that can be run on a variety of platforms. To be interpreted and executed by the CPU, the code will need to be translated.

Widgets

A **widget** is a graphical user interface (GUI) element that displays information or allows a user to interact with the operating system or an application in a specific way. Icons, pull-down menus, buttons, selection boxes, progress indicators, checkboxes, scroll bars, windows, window edges (which allow you to resize the window), toggle buttons, forms, and a variety of other devices for displaying information and inviting, accepting, and responding to user actions are all examples of widgets.

"Widgets" also refers to the little programs that are developed to define how a particular widget looks, operates, and responds to user actions in programming. Most operating systems provide a set of ready-to-use widgets that a programmer can use to customize an application's behavior, but it is also possible to develop new widgets.

Algorithm

A set of instructions used to solve a problem is referred to as an **algorithm**. It's the cognitive process of a computer.

Coding

Coding is the process of creating computer instructions. Programs, like people, speak a variety of languages. Roblox, for example, makes use of the Lua programming language, whereas Minecraft was created using Java.

Languages

Coding **languages** are used by computers to understand what people want them to do. People communicate with computers in languages like C++ or Java, just as they communicate with each other in English or Japanese. JavaScript and Python are two of the most popular coding languages.

JavaScript

JavaScript (or Java) is a multi-platform computer programming language with a lot of capabilities. It's used in a wide range of professional and commercial applications, including every Android app as well as the Android operating system. Markus Persson developed Minecraft entirely in Java. Gmail was built in Java, because it has a high performance rate and a solid web architecture.

Python

Python is another programming language that is currently gaining in popularity with each new library introduced to its collection. It takes care of everything from web development and game creation, to machine learning and artificial intelligence. Python is also renowned for having a simpler syntax than most other programming languages, including Java and C++.

Mobile App Development Methodologies

When creating mobile applications, there are four key development methodologies to consider.

- **Native Apps for Mobile**
- **Mobile Hybrid Applications**
- **Progressive Web Applications (PWAs)**
- **Cross-Platform Mobile Applications**

Each of these techniques to mobile app development has its own set of benefits and drawbacks. As a developer, before you decide the best development method for your projects from the above, you should assess the intended user experience, native features required by the application, your budget allocation, time estimate, and available resources for the upkeep of the app. This way, you will be able to make a more informed decision and maximise your chosen technique to effectively execute your design.

Native Mobile Applications

Native apps are created in the platform owner's programming language and frameworks. They run directly on the device's operating system, such as iOS or Android.

Hybrid Mobile Applications

Hybrid apps are bundled as app installation packages and constructed with conventional web technologies like JavaScript, CSS, and HTML5. Hybrid apps, unlike native apps, run on a 'web container,' which includes a browser runtime as well as a bridge to native device APIs via Apache Cordova.

Progressive Web Applications

Progressive web apps (PWAs) are web applications that leverage a set of browser features to give an 'app-like' user experience, such as working offline, running a background process, and providing a link to the device's home screen. By avoiding app store delivery and installation, PWAs provide an alternative to standard mobile app development by taking advantage of a set of browser features.

Cross-Platform Development

The process of developing an app that runs across many platforms is referred to as **cross-platform development**. Cross-platform mobile apps can be developed in a variety of programming languages and frameworks, but they are compiled into native apps that run directly on the device's operating system. The resulting apps can be used on both Android and iOS.

Prior to the creation of cross-platform mobile applications, developers had to design individual application codes for each platform in order to develop standards-compliant applications. These are referred to as native apps. The process was quite tasking, because each coding process required a codebase (and a different programmer) for iOS (iPhone) as well as separate codebase (and developer) for Android. Objective-C and Swift are the standard programming languages for native iOS, while Java and Kotlin work best for native Android development.

As you may expect, this development strategy complicates things for a variety of reasons.

- Keeping two sets of code in sync is inconvenient. Simply said, whenever a developer modified the iPhone code for whatever reason, they had to change the Android code to match.
- It was too expensive, because you needed developers with multiple skill sets.
- The app for one platform could seem very different from the app for the other platforms.

Early Cross-Platform Development Tools

Various IT teams began the race to develop their firms' mobile applications as fast and efficiently as possible, a task complicated by the need to support both iOS and Android devices. As a result, many businesses began to work on cross-platform mobile development tools, which would allow them to create apps for both iOS and Android using the same code base. They immediately separated the development tools into two categories: those that used native libraries and those that did not.

Native Libraries-Based Development Tools

On top of Apple and Google's original SDKs, these tools produced a "Unified" API. Many of these development tools are still available, such as Xamarin, Appcelerator, and Nativescript. The difficulty with these kinds of apps is that the "Unified API" doesn't cover everything, leaving developers with a lot of work to do, such as writing platform-specific code. These apps also make use of the SDK's Widgets. As a result, the apps may differ in appearance due to the use of various Widgets from various sources.

Tools That Didn't Rely on Native Libraries

These development tools adopted a unique methodology. The majority of them attempted to avoid using the SDK by writing code that ran in the platform's browser. This allowed the programmer to take advantage of many of the HTML5 and JavaScript features that were already available. The program would be displayed on a web browser. A "webview" is a browser embedded into a mobile application, resulting in a hybrid app. Using a webview, mobile apps can be developed using web technologies (HTML, JavaScript, CSS, and so on) while still being packaged as a native app and distributed through the app store.

The issue with these applications is that they are slow. They're not executing in compiled machine code; instead, they use a disguised web browser. Many of these development tools are still in use, such as Cordova and PhoneGap.

Modern Cross-Platform Development Tools

Today, based on extensive market research and real-world examples from prominent organizations, several players have emerged to make your job easier and give your project a competitive edge. These are some of the major leaders in the field of mobile app development tools:

Ionic

Drifty Co.'s Max Lynch, Ben Sperry, and Adam Bradley launched **Ionic**, a comprehensive open-source SDK for hybrid mobile app development, in 2013. Ionic apps are written in web-standard languages such as HTML, CSS, and JavaScript. As a result, if you can create a basic web app, you can build with Ionic as well. You can create a native iOS or Android app, a native desktop app, or a web app using Ionic, all from a single codebase.

Iconic enables developers to create high-performing iOS and Android apps, thanks to strong community support and large libraries of native components. With Ionic's web usage metrics, designers are compelled to use this architecture to build local applications and progressive web applications. It is an open-source framework that allows a programmer to use a library of portable upgraded reusable UI segments, motions, and devices to intelligently connect with applications in a short time span.

React Native

React Native is a JavaScript framework that allows the programmer to create native apps for iOS and Android. It's built on the React JavaScript library, which was created by Facebook. It was released back in March of 2015 and very quickly gained popularity among developers. React Native enables you to write modules in a variety of languages, including C++, Java, Swift, Objective-C, and Python. The nicest thing is that it's built on JavaScript, which the majority of developers are already familiar with. Furthermore, because React Native is an open-source framework that allows you to reuse the codebase for application advancement, planning the program with it is fast and pleasant for the designers.

The idea of developing apps for all platforms using only one model seems far-fetched. React Native meets this need by speeding up the process of developing apps for numerous platforms, because it allows much of the code to be reused across them. It's popular because it works equally well on mobile and non-mobile websites. React Native is similar to React, but instead of using web components as building blocks, it employs native components. Facebook, Facebook Ads, Walmart, Bloomberg, Instagram, SoundCloud Pulse, Townske, Gyroscope, and Wix are among the most well-known React Native apps.

Components in React Native are pure, side-effect-free functions that return the state of the views at any given time. As a result, writing state-dependent views is easy because you don't have to worry about updating the view when the state changes—the framework does it for you. Because the UI is produced using genuine native views, the end user experience isn't as poor as with alternative solutions that simply put a web component inside a WebView.

Developers employ **component** objects to create user interfaces. These components may have software that allows them to respond to user input and provide an interactive user interface. The way it works, React Native runs in two parts:

- **The user interface (UI):** This component shows the user interface and receives user input.
- **The JavaScript interpreter:** The JavaScript application code is interpreted and executed. A bridge connects the two halves.

Pros

- The React Native framework is a fantastic tool. It has the distinct advantage of being the more established player, having been released in 2015.
- Because it comes with so many ready-to-use components,

React Native is an easy-to-learn and tremendously productive tool.

Cons

- React Native apps aren't fully compiled in the native environment.
- Although much of the deployed code is native, your section of the app runs as embedded JavaScript and communicates with the native components via a bridge. This isn't the best option in terms of performance.

Google Flutter

Flutter is a Google-developed open-source UI software development kit that allows developers to construct native-looking iOS and Android apps using a single codebase. Google introduced Flutter in 2017, and it has since been used to create over 100,000 apps. It is used to create cross-platform applications from a single codebase for Android, iOS, Linux, Mac, Windows, Google Fuchsia, and the web.

Flutter is causing a stir, because it offers a novel approach to cross-platform mobile app development. It has a large number of UI components and gadgets, as well as a powerful delivery motor, allowing designers to make changes to the app with ease. Instead of using the native iOS or Android UI widgets that come with their retrospective SDKs, you write user interfaces using Google Flutter user interface widgets.

Flutter is made up of two main components:

- **An SDK (Software Development Kit):** A set of tools that will assist you in the development of your applications. Tools for compiling your code into native machine code are also included here (for iOS and Android).

- **A Framework (Widget-based UI Library):** A set of customizable reusable user interface elements (buttons, text inputs, sliders, and so on).

It uses the same Widgets from the same library, and so a Flutter app created with Flutter Widgets will look the same on iOS and Android. Many widgets are included in Flutter, including those that mirror Google's Material design and those that mimic Apple's iOS design.

These widgets are drawn using Google Flutter's own high-performance rendering engine and are meant to function across all mobile platforms. These widgets can also be customized. You create the application code in Google's Dart language, which is turned into machine code ahead of time for native-like performance, giving it an edge over React Native. Here, between the user interface and the application code, there is no link. The one obvious disadvantage is that developers will have to learn Dart rather than reusing their existing JavaScript skills.

Pros

- Easy to use and learn. Flutter is a contemporary framework that makes it easier to design mobile apps. If you've worked with Java, Swift, or React Native, you'll see how unique Flutter is. You can make a true native app without writing any code.
- You can make changes to your code and see the consequences right away. It's known as Hot-Reload. After you save, it simply takes a few moments for the application to be updated.
- Because you don't have to design and manage two mobile apps, developing a mobile app with Flutter is less expensive. You can also quickly personalize widgets offered by Flutter to build a valuable user interface for your consumers.
- Documentation is excellent. Flutter's documentation has a lot to offer, and everything is quite detailed with simple examples for fundamental use cases.

- Android Studio and VS Code both support it. Android Studio is a full-featured program that includes everything you need. VS Code is a little program with a lot of customization options thanks to marketplace plugins.
- Flutter offers a command-line utility called Flutter Doctor that can help developers get started. It checks which tools are installed and which need to be configured on the local machine. You can proceed with constructing a new Flutter app after the Flutter Doctor command is satisfied. To get started with Flutter, there's a separate page that explains how to set up the editors. Once this is done, you can proceed to create a new Flutter app from the command line.

Conclusion

When it comes to reducing application development costs, development time, and market time, a large number of SMEs, new businesses, and even multimillion-dollar ventures are opting for cross-stage models for their next application development project. Google Flutter appears to be the best solution right now if you want to develop performant cross-platform mobile web applications.

THREE

Introduction To Dart

Dart is a Google-created general-purpose programming language released in 2011. The technical envelope of a language—that is, the collective decisions made during development that influence the language's capabilities and strengths—defines it. Dart is optimized for client development, prioritizing both development (sub-second stateful hot reload) and high-quality production experiences across a wide range of compilation targets (web, mobile, and desktop). Dart is an open-source general-purpose programming language with a syntax comparable to that of C.

It's a C-style object-oriented language that supports programming concepts such as interfaces and classes. It's one of the best languages for creating quick apps on any platform, because it's client-oriented. Its purpose is to provide the most productive programming language for cross-platform development, as well as a versatile runtime platform for app frameworks.

Dart is also the backbone of Flutter. Dart not only powers Flutter apps with its language and runtimes, but it also helps developers with formatting, analyzing, and testing code. Data structures like arrays, generics, and optional typing can be replicated with Dart collections.

The following data types are supported by the Dart language.

- **Numbers:** Used to represent integer and double numeric literals.
- **Strings:** A string is a collection of characters. Single or double quotations are used to specify string values.
- **Booleans:** The **bool** keyword in Dart is used to represent Boolean values such as true and false. It is also used to represent a collection of objects in lists and maps.
- **Decision Making and Loops:** Before the instructions are executed, a decision making block examines a condition. **If**, **If..else**, and **switch** statements are all supported in Dart. Loops are used to repeatedly run a section of code until a certain condition is met. Dart supports loops like **for**, **for..in**, **while**, and **do..while**. They can be defined as a method, similar to our void function, and they operate like first-class objects, which means they can be saved in variables, supplied as arguments, and returned as a normal function return value.

Dart: The Language

The Dart programming language is type-safe: it employs static type checking to ensure that a variable's value always corresponds to the static type of the variable. This is referred to as "sound typing." Dart's typing system is also versatile, allowing for the use of a dynamic type mixed with runtime checks, which can be beneficial for experimentation or for code that requires a lot of dynamic behavior.

If you execute a Dart program without null safety, the call **to.length** raises a **NoSuchMethodError** error. The **Null** class has no "length" getter, and the null value is an instance of it.

Failures in the runtime are a pain. This is particularly true in a language like Dart, which is intended to run on a user's device. You can usually restart a server application before anyone sees it has failed. Users, on the other hand, are not pleased when a Flutter app crashes on their phone. You're not happy if your customers aren't happy.

Dart has good null safety, which means that values can't be null unless you say so. Through this, Dart protects users from null exceptions at execution. Non-nullability is preserved at runtime if you view your running code in the debugger.

Dart Native (machine code JIT and AOT)

Dart features both a Dart VM with just-in-time (JIT) compilation and an ahead-of-time (AOT) compiler for producing machine code for programs targeting mobile and desktop platforms. Iteration requires a quick development cycle. A just-in-time compiler (JIT) with incremental recompilation (allowing hot reload), live metrics collectors (powering DevTools), and sophisticated debugging capabilities are all available in the Dart VM.

The Dart AOT compiler enables ahead-of-time compilation to native ARM or x64 computer code when applications are ready for deployment, whether to an app store or a production backend. Your AOT-compiled program starts up quickly and consistently. It operates inside a fast Dart runtime that both executes the sound Dart type system and maintains memory. This is done with a generational garbage collector and quick object allocation.

Platforms

Dart offers a development time compiler (**dartdevc**) as well as a production time compiler for web projects (**dart2js**). Dart is translated into JavaScript by both compilers. Unlike traditional languages, Dart has been optimized to run as JavaScript, as an interpreted application, or as a native application within a web browser.

Within a Web Browser

Dart comes with an SDK that includes command-line tools for converting Dart source code to JavaScript. This has been done so well that the resulting transpiled JavaScript is faster than its hand-coded counterpart. By going to dartpad.dartlang.org, you may try out Dart on your web browser. You have the option of writing your own code or running the sample code.

A word of caution: some Dart functionalities will not run properly from a browser. For instance, you may find that you cannot read from **stdin** or accept user input.

As Interpreted Application

A Virtual Machine is included in the Dart SDK. This works as a virtual sandbox, within which code can run without having to interact directly with the operating system. This process makes it easy for a Dart code to be executed from the command line using the SDK's **dart** command line tool. The code is compiled just-in-time as it is executed. Through these means, you can write your server-side apps easily because, here, Dart performs in the same manner as Java/.Net.

As Native Application

Here, Dart code can be compiled in advance and distributed as machine code. When a developer runs a Dart program from the command line, the JIT compiler can reload the code when the underlying source code changes, while maintaining the variables as much as feasible. As a result, the developer can simultaneously write and run code, because the application development is extremely quick. After the development process, the code can be compiled and deployed as a native program using the ahead-of-time compiler.

Dart SDK

The Dart SDK includes all of the libraries and command line tools needed to create Dart command line, server, and non-Flutter web projects. The Dart SDK is located in the Flutter SDK's **bin/cache/dart-sdk** subdirectory. It will be downloaded the first time you execute the **flutter** command—so if you already have Flutter installed, you may not need to download the Dart SDK separately. If any of the following statements are true, you should consider downloading the Dart SDK:

- Flutter isn't something you utilize.
- You're using a version of Flutter that's older than 1.21.
- You want to save disk space or download time, but you don't need Flutter for your application.

Command-line tools, **Command-line compilers**, and **Libraries** are its three basic components.

Command Line Tools

The Dart command line interface allows you to write, format, analyze, test, compile, and run Dart programs. This includes the following:

- **dart:** This command allows you to run a Dart file in the Dart Virtual Machine.
- **dart2js:** This is a program that converts Dart source code to JavaScript.
- **dartanalyser:** This is a program that analyzes Dart source code. Many code editors employ this technique to highlight errors and warnings.
- **dartdevc:** This is a program that converts Dart source code to JavaScript. It's similar to dart2js, except it allows for incremental compilation, which is useful for developers.
- **dartdoc:** This is a tool that generates documentation for Dart from source code.
- **dartfmt:** This is a very useful program because it provides dart formatting to Dart source code.

Command-Line Compilers

Dart may be run without being compiled to JavaScript in a browser called **Dartium**. Dartium is essentially Chrome with a Dart virtual machine. The popular Dart web development path, on the other hand, now involves writing code in Dart and compiling and running it as JavaScript using the dart2js and dartdevc JavaScript compilers, as well as the webdev and build runner utilities.

When creating your app, webdev prefers dartdevc because it provides incremental compilation, allowing you to see the results of your changes fast. When it comes to deploying your project, webdev recommends dart2js, which uses techniques like tree shaking to generate efficient code. More information can be found here:

https://webdev.dartlang.org/tools/webdev

Dart Core libraries

Dart includes a large set of core libraries that cover a wide range of programming tasks.

- Every Dart application has built-in types, collections, and other essential functions (**dart:core**)
- Queues, linked lists, hashmaps, and binary trees are more advanced collection types (**dart:collection**)
- Converting between multiple data representations, such as JSON and UTF-8, with encoders and decoders (**dart:convert**)
- Random number creation and mathematical constants and functions (**dart:math**)
- Non-web apps can use file, socket, HTTP, and other I/O methods (**dart:io**)
- Future and Stream classes provide asynchronous programming support (**dart:async**)

- Fixed-size data (for example, unsigned 8-byte integers) and SIMD numeric types (**dart:typed data**) are effectively handled by lists.
- For interoperability with other code that uses a C-style interface, foreign function interfaces are used (**dart:ffi**)
- Isolates—autonomous workers that are comparable to threads but don't share memory and communicate exclusively through messages—are used in concurrent programming (**dart:isolate**)
- For web-based applications that need to communicate with the browser and the Document Object Model (DOM), HTML elements and other resources are available (**dart:html**)

Many APIs are offered by a comprehensive set of packages in addition to the core libraries. Many important extra packages are available from the Dart project, including characters, intl, http, crypto, and markdown. Thousands of packages with support for XML, Windows integration, SQLite, and compression are also available from third-party publishers and the greater community.

Flutter Development

As you learned in the previous chapter, the Flutter framework is an impressive UI toolkit that runs on iOS, Android, macOS, Windows, Linux, and the web and is driven by the Dart platform. It includes tooling and UI libraries for creating UI experiences that operate on iOS, Android, macOS, Windows, Linux, and the web.

Flutter was primarily built in Dart and operates on native platforms. As a result, Flutter is both quick and adaptable, as the Flutter widgets were written in Dart. Most often, when developing a Flutter application, you run it in **Debug Mode**, and your code is JIT compiled and interpreted. The 'check' or 'slow' mode is the name for this mode. The assertion functions, including all debugging information, service extensions, and debugging aids like "observatory," are available in this mode.

This mode is designed for quick development and operation but not for speed of execution, package size, or deployment. Once your app is complete, you can compile it to run in **Release Mode** as a native application, which will significantly improve its performance. We will discuss this in greater detail later in the book.

Advanced Dart With Examples

DartPad

As you now know, Flutter—Google's UI toolkit for building attractive, natively-built mobile, web, and desktop apps from a single codebase—uses Dart as its programming language. You may easily build and run your examples in **DartPad** as long as you have a stable browser. DartPad is a free, open-source tool that allows you to experiment with Dart's capabilities and core libraries in any modern browser. It takes a new approach to features that Java developers may not be familiar with.

DartPad additionally supports the **package:flutter** and **dart:ui** libraries when creating Flutter apps. DartPad does not support any libraries or deferred loading, and it does not allow you to use packages from the pub package repository. You can, however, use an IDE like WebStorm or IntelliJ with the Dart plugin—or Visual Studio Code with the Dart Code extension—if you please.

The above is what DartPad looks like when configured to run Dart.

Try running some samples and developing a small command line app with DartPad by following these simple steps:

- Go to dartPad.dev to get started.
- On the left, you'll see Dart code, and on the right, you'll see a spot for the output.
- Using the Samples list in the upper right, select a Flutter sample like Sunflower. To the right is the rendered output.

You can use New Pad to write a simple command-line app in these steps:

1. Confirm that you want to discard changes to the existing pad by clicking the **New Pad** button.

2. After clicking the **Dart logo**, make sure HTML support is turned off, and then click **Create**.

3. Make a code change. Change the **main()** function to include the following code:

```
for (var char in 'hello'.split('')) {
print(char);
}
```

4. DartPad displays hints, documentation, and autocomplete suggestions as you type.

5. Select **Format** from the drop-down menu. DartPad employs the Dart formatter to ensure appropriate indentation, white space, and line wrapping in your code.

6. Start your app.

7. Try adding a bug if you didn't have any while entering the code. If you alter “split” to “spit,” for example, you’ll get warnings at the bottom right of the window. When you launch the app, the terminal displays a compilation error.

DartPad’s language features and APIs are dependent on the Dart SDK version that it is currently using. This SDK version can be seen in DartPad’s bottom right corner. DartPad can also be embedded in web pages and customized to fit your needs.

Dart Language Samples

This compilation isn’t extensive; it’s just a quick overview of the language for those of you who, like me, prefer to learn by doing.

Hello World

The **main()** function is present in every program. You can use the top-level **print()** method to display text on the console:

```
void main() {
print('Hello, World!');
}
```

Variables

Here's a sample of how to generate and initialize a variable:

```
var name = 'Bob';
```

Variables are used to keep track of references. The **name** variable holds a reference to a **String** object with the value "Bob." The name variable's type is assumed to be String, but you can alter it by specifying it. Specify the Object type if an object isn't bound to a single type.

```
Object name = 'Bob';
```

Default Value

Uninitialized variables that have a nullable type have an initial value of null. (Every variable has a nullable type if you haven't enabled null safety.) Because numbers, like everything else in Dart, are objects, even numeric variables start out null.

```
int? lineCount;
assert(lineCount == null);
```

The **assert()** call is ignored by production code. If the condition is false during development, however, **assert(condition)** produces an exception. If null safety is enabled, you must set the values of non-nullable variables before using them:

```
int lineCount = 0;
```

A local variable does not need to be initialized where it is declared, but it must be assigned a value before it can be used. Since Dart can detect that **lineCount** is non-null by the time it's supplied to **print()**, the following code is valid:

```
int lineCount;

if (weLikeToCount) {
lineCount = countLines();
} else {
lineCount = 0;
}

print(lineCount);
```

Late Variables

The late modifier was created in Dart 2.12 and it has two major uses: declaring a non-nullable variable that will be initialized later, and lazily initializing a variable.

Declaring A Non-nullable Variable That Will Be Initialized Later

Dart's control flow analysis can usually detect whether a non-nullable variable is set to a non-null value before it's used, but this detection isn't always made. Top-level variables and instance variables are two frequent examples: Dart can't always tell if they're set, so in some cases it doesn't try. If you're certain a variable gets set before it's used, but Dart disputes, you can resolve the issue by declaring the variable as late:

```
late String description;

void main() {

description = 'Feijoada!';

print(description);

}
```

Lazy Initialization

When a late variable is utilized without being properly initialized, a runtime error occurs. If you declare a variable late but initialize it at its declaration, the initializer executes the first time the variable is used. This lazy initialization is useful in a few situations:

- Where the variable may not be required, and initializing it is expensive.
- If you're setting up an instance variable, and the variable's initializer requires access to this.

Built-in Types

The Dart programming language offers additional functionality for each of the following:

- Numbers (**int**, **double**)
- Strings (**string**)
- Booleans (**bool**)
- Lists (**list**; also known as arrays)
- Sets (**set**)
- Maps (**map**)

- Runes (**runes**; often replaced by the characters API)
- Symbols (**symbol**)
- The value null (**null**)

The ability to create objects using literals is part of this specific capability. A good example of a string literal is "this is a string," while a boolean literal is "true."

You can typically use constructors to initialize variables in Dart, since every variable relates to an object as a class instance. There are constructors for several of the built-in kinds. To make a map, for example, you can use the **Map()** constructor. Other types play key roles in the Dart language, as well.

- **Object:** Except for Null, Object is the superclass of all Dart classes.
- **Future and Stream:** Used to support asynchrony.
- **Iterable:** This type of variable is used in for-in loops and synchronous generator functions.
- **Never:** Indicates that an expression will never be able to complete its evaluation.
- **Dynamic:** Indicates that static checking should be disabled. In most cases, **Object** or **Object?** should be used instead.
- **Void:** A value is never used when it is set to void. This is frequently used as a return type.
- **Numbers (Num):** Dart numbers are divided into two types: integers and doubles.

Integers (int)

Numbers without a decimal point are known as integers. Depending on the platform, integer values of no more than 64 bits are allowed. Values for native systems range from -2^{63} to $2^{63}-1$. Integer values range from -2^{53} to $2^{53}-1$ and are represented on the web as JavaScript numbers (64-bit floating-point values with no fractional portion).

Doubles

A number is a double if it contains a decimal. The IEEE 754 standard specifies 64-bit (double-precision) floating-point numbers.

Basic operators such as **+**, **-**, **/**, and ***** are included in the **num** type, as are **abs()**, **ceil()**, and **floor()**, among other ways. (The **int** class defines bitwise operators such as **>>**.) The **dart:math** library may have what you're seeking for if num and its subtypes don't. Here are some instances of integer literal definitions:

```
var x = 1;

var hex = 0xDEADBEEF;

var exponent = 8e5;
```

Here are some examples of double literal definitions:

```
var y = 1.1;

var exponents = 1.42e5;
```

A variable can also be declared as a number. When this happens, the variable could have both integer and double values, as shown below:

```
num x = 1; // x can have both int and double values
x += 2.5;
```

Integer literals can be converted to doubles when necessary:

```
double z = 1; // Equivalent to double z = 1.0.
```

A string can also be converted into a number, and vice versa:

```
// String -> int
var one = int.parse('1');
assert(one == 1);
// String -> double
var onePointOne = double.parse('1.1');
assert(onePointOne == 1.1);
// int -> String
String oneAsString = 1.toString();
assert(oneAsString == '1');
// double -> String
```

```
String piAsString = 3.14159.toStringAsFixed(2);

assert(piAsString == '3.14');
```

Booleans

Dart contains a type called **bool** that represents boolean values. The boolean literals *true* and *false*, which are both compile-time constants, are the only objects of type bool. As a result of Dart's type safety, you can't use **if (nonbooleanValue)** or **assert (nonbooleanValue)**. Instead, check for values explicitly, as in:

```
// Check for an empty string.

var fullName = '';

assert(fullName.isEmpty);

// Check for zero.

var hitPoints = 0;

assert(hitPoints <= 0);

// Check for null.

var unicorn;

assert(unicorn == null);

// Check for NaN.

var iMeantToDoThis = 0 / 0;

assert(iMeantToDoThis.isNaN);
```

Lists

The array, or ordered group of things, is perhaps the most common collection in practically every programming language. Arrays are **list** objects in Dart, so most people just refer to them as lists. Dart list literals resemble JavaScript array literals in appearance. Here's a quick list in Dart:

```
var list = [1, 2, 3];
```

Dart deduces that the list is of type **List<int>**. The analyzer or runtime throws an error if you try to add non-integer objects to this list. The spread operator **(...)** and the null-aware spread operator **(...?)** were added in Dart 2.3, and they provide a simple way to insert several values into a collection. To insert all the values of a list into another list, for example, you can use the spread operator **(...)**:

```
var list = [1, 2, 3];

var list2 = [0, ...list];

assert(list2.length == 4);
```

If you surmise that the expression to the right of the spread operator might be null, use a null-aware spread operator **(...?)** to avoid exceptions:

```
var list;
var list2 = [0, ...?list];
assert(list2.length == 1);
```

Dart also has the **collection if** and **collection for** functions, which you may use to create collections with conditionals **(if)** and repetition **(for)**. Here's an example of how to use collection to make a three- or four-item list:

```
var nav = [
'Home',
'Furniture',
'Plants',
if (promoActive) 'Outlet'
];
```

Sets

In Dart, a **set** is an unordered collection of unique items. Set literals and the Set type provide support for sets. Below is a basic Dart set made with a set literal:

```
var halogens = {'fluorine', 'chlorine', 'bromine', 'iodine',
'astatine'};
```

Dart deduces that halogens are of the **Set<String>** type. The analyzer or runtime will raise an error if you try to add the improper type of value to the set. You can use {} followed by a type argument to generate an empty set, or assign {} to a variable of type Set as seen below:

```
var names = <String>{};

// Set<String> names = {}; // This works, too.

// var names = {}; // Creates a map
```

Note that map literals have a syntax that is similar to set literals. Map literals came first and so {} defaults to the Map type. Dart produces an object of type **Map<dynamic, dynamic>** for cases where one forgets the type annotation on {} or the variable it's assigned to.

Maps

A map is an object that associates keys and values in general. Any type of object can be used as both a key and a value. Each key appears just once—however, the same value can be used several times. Map literals and the Map type in Dart enable support for maps. Here are a number of examples of simple Dart maps made with map literals:

```
var gifts = {
// Key: Value
'first': 'partridge',
'second': 'turtledoves',
'fifth': 'golden rings'
};

var nobleGases = {
2: 'helium',
10: 'neon',
18: 'argon',
};
```

In Dart, **gifts** has the type **Map<String, String>**, while **nobleGases** has the type **Map<int, String>**. The analyzer or runtime will raise an error if you try to add the improper kind of value to either map.

Runes and Grapheme Clusters

Runes in Dart reveal a string's Unicode code points. Unicode (extended) grapheme clusters are user-perceived characters which can be viewed and manipulated with the characters package. Each letter, digit, and symbol used in all of the world's writing systems has a unique numeric value defined by Unicode. Since a Dart string is made up of UTF-16 code units, expressing Unicode code points within it necessitates the use of specific syntax.

A Unicode code point is usually written as \uXXXX, where XXXX is a four-digit hexadecimal value. The heart character (♥) is, for example, \u2665. Place the value in curly brackets to specify more or fewer than four hex digits. The laughing emoji (😆) is, for example, \u{1f606}. Use the characters getter defined on String by the characters package if you need to read or write specific Unicode characters. The string as a succession of grapheme clusters is returned as a character object. Here's an example of how the characters API can be used:

```
import 'package:characters/characters.dart';

...

var hi = 'Hi 🇩🇰';

print(hi);

print('The end of the string: ${hi.substring(hi.length - 1)}');

print('The last character: ${hi.characters.last}\n');
```

Depending on your conditions, the output should look like this:

```
$ dart bin/main.dart

Hi 🇩🇰

The end of the string: ???

The last character: 🇩🇰
```

Symbols

An operator or identifier declared in a Dart program is represented by a **symbol** object. You may never need to utilize symbols, but they're essential for APIs that refer to identifiers by name. This is because minification only affects the names of identifiers, not the symbols. Compile-time constants are symbol literals. You can use a symbol literal, which is just **#** followed by the identifier, to retrieve the symbol for an identifier:

```
#radix

#bar
```

Functions

Dart is an object-oriented programming language. This means that functions can be provided as arguments to other functions or allocated to variables. Here's an example of how to execute a function:

```
bool isNoble(int atomicNumber) {

return _nobleGases[atomicNumber] != null;

}
```

You can use a shorthand syntax for functions that only have one expression:

```
bool isNoble(int atomicNumber) =>
_nobleGases[atomicNumber] != null;
```

The **=> expr** syntax (also known as the arrow syntax) is a shorthand for { **return expr;** }. Only an expression can exist between the arrow **(=>)** and the semicolon **(;)**. You can't use an if-statement there, for instance, but you can use a conditional expression.

Parameters

A function can have as many positional parameters as it needs. Named parameters *or* optional positional parameters can be added after these—but not *both*. Even with necessary parameters, some APIs, such as Flutter widget constructors, employ just named parameters. When passing arguments to a function or defining function parameters, you can use trailing commas.

Named Parameters

Unless they're explicitly declared as mandatory, named parameters are optional. You can use **paramName: value** to specify named parameters when calling a function. Consider the following scenario:

```
enableFlags(bold: true, hidden: false);
```

When defining a function, you also typically use **{param1, param2, ...}** to specify the named parameters, if any:

```
/// Sets the [bold] and [hidden] flags ...
void enableFlags({bool? bold, bool? hidden
```

Default Parameter Values

Your function can use **=** to define default values for either named or positional parameters. Compile-time constants must be used as default values. The default value is null if no default value is specified. Setting default values for named parameters can be done in the following way:

```
/// Sets the [bold] and [hidden] flags ...
void enableFlags({bool bold = false, bool hidden = false}) {...}

// bold will be true; hidden will be false.
enableFlags(bold: true);
```

Every program must have a top-level **main()** function that acts as the app's entry point. The **main()** function returns void and has an optional **List<String>** parameter for arguments. Here's a simple **main()** function:

```
void main() {
print('Hello, World!');
}
```

For command line apps that take arguments, here's an illustration of a **main**() function:

```
// Run the app like this: dart args.dart 1 test
void main(List<String> arguments) {
print(arguments);

assert(arguments.length == 2);
assert(int.parse(arguments[0]) == 1);
assert(arguments[1] == 'test');
}
```

Anonymous Functions

The majority of functions, such as **main()** and **printElement**, are named (). An anonymous function, often known as a lambda or closure, is a type of nameless function. You can use an anonymous function to add or delete items from a collection by assigning it to a variable.

An anonymous function has zero or more parameters, separated by commas and optional type annotations, and is enclosed in parentheses.

The body of the function is included in the code block as follows:

([[Type] param1[, …]]) { codeBlock;};

The example below shows how to create an anonymous function with an untyped parameter, item. The function prints a string that includes the value at the provided index for each item in the list:

```
const list = ['apples', 'bananas', 'oranges'];

list.forEach((item) {

print('${list.indexOf(item)}: $item');

});
```

You can use the arrow notation to shorten à function that has only one expression or return statement. When sending anonymous functions as arguments, this shorthand syntax can be incredibly helpful:

```
flybyObjects.where((name)                                   =>
name.contains('turn')).forEach(print);
```

Classes

A **class** of three attributes, two constructors, and a function is shown below. Since one of the attributes can't be set directly, a getter method is used to specify it (instead of a variable).

```
class Spacecraft {

String name;

DateTime? launchDate;

int? get launchYear => launchDate?.year; // read-only non-final property

// Constructor, with syntactic sugar for assignment to members.

Spacecraft(this.name, this.launchDate) {

// Initialization code goes here.

}

// Named constructor that forwards to the default one.

Spacecraft.unlaunched(String name) : this(name, null);

// Method.

void describe() {

print('Spacecraft: $name');

var launchDate = this.launchDate; // Type promotion doesn't work on getters.

if (launchDate != null) {

int years = DateTime.now().difference(launchDate).inDays ~/ 365;

print('Launched: $launchYear ($years years ago)');

} else {

print('Unlaunched');

}
```

```
}
}
```

Mixins

Mixins allow code to be reused across several class hierarchies. A mixin declaration looks like this:

```
mixin Piloted {
int astronauts = 1;

void describeCrew() {
print('Number of astronauts: $astronauts');
}
}
```

Simply extend the class with the mixin to add the mixin's features:

```
class PilotedCraft extends Spacecraft with Piloted {
// ···
}
```

Interfaces and Abstract Classes

There is no interface keyword in the Dart programming language. All classes, on the other hand, specify an interface automatically. As a result, any class can be implemented:

```
class MockSpaceship implements Spacecraft {
// ···
}
```

You can design an abstract class that a concrete class can extend (or implement), and abstract methods can be found in abstract classes (with empty bodies). The **describeWithEmphasis()** function is available in any class that extends Describable and invokes the extender's version of **describe()**:

```
abstract class Describable {
void describe();

void describeWithEmphasis() {
print('=========');
describe();
print('=========');
}
}
```

Async

While working with Dart, you can use async and await to make your code more legible:

```
const oneSecond = Duration(seconds: 1);

// ···

Future<void> printWithDelay(String message) async {

await Future.delayed(oneSecond);

print(message);

}

The above is identical to:

Future<void> printWithDelay(String message) {

return Future.delayed(oneSecond).then((_) {

print(message);

});

}
```

As shown in the following example, **async** and **await** make asynchronous programming easier to read:

```
Future<void> createDescriptions(Iterable<String> objects) async
{
for (var object in objects) {
try {
var file = File('$object.txt');
if (await file.exists()) {
var modified = await file.lastModified();
print(
'File for $object already exists. It was modified on $modified.');
continue;
}
await file.create();
await file.writeAsString('Start describing $object in this file.');
} on IOException catch (e) {
print('Cannot create description for $object: $e');
}
}
}
```

Conclusion

Even though this chapter summarises some of the most commonly used features in the Dart language, there are lots more features being implemented. For more information, visit these pages.

For Dart language specification: dart.dev/guides/language/spec

For effective Dart: dart.dev/guides/language/effective-dart

To learn more about Dart's core libraries: dart.dev/guides/libraries/library-tour

FOUR

Introduction To Flutter

The purpose of this chapter is to give you a more intimate understanding of Flutter before you get into installing and using it.

What is Flutter?

Flutter is not a programming language (like JavaScript, for example). It is a Google mobile SDK/UI framework that allows developers to create native apps for Android and iOS devices. Developers build code that works on both platforms in a single codebase.

Flutter uses existing code and so is readily available to developers around the world. It is the only mobile SDK framework that supports reactive styles without the use of a JavaScript bridge. The SDK is open-source and free, allowing developers to experiment with and create powerful tracking applications. This is the reason why Flutter-based apps and interfaces exist. Flutter uses a single codebase, compiles directly to native arm code, takes advantage of the GPU, and makes use of the platform APIs and services.

Today's mobile users expect gorgeous designs, smooth animations, and quick performance from their apps. As a result, developers are expected to meet these goals without sacrificing quality or performance. They turn to Flutter for the following reasons.

High Productivity

Flutter was created with the goal of speeding up the development of apps. It is substantially faster than other development methods and does not require a Javascript bridge. You can make changes to your code and then hot reload to see your changes in action immediately. Flutter comes with all of the UI Widgets you'll need and is compatible with most IDEs.

Saves Time

You may utilize the same codebase for your iOS and Android apps, because Flutter is cross-platform. This will undoubtedly save you time and money.

Exceptional Quality

Flutter comes with a wide range of widgets that can be customized for Android, iOS, and Material Design. Flutter's work with Google's Material Design has resulted in a strong UI experience that is simple to construct. This aids in the creation of a smooth, crisp, and refined app experience similar to that of a native app.

The Flutter UI Widgets that come with the project function fluidly and normally with the target platform. The target system's scrolling, navigation, icons, and typefaces are all compatible. When you use the Flutter Widgets to create an Android app, it appears to be a standard Android app. When you use the Flutter Widgets to create an iOS app, it appears to be a standard iOS app. See the figure below for the demo:

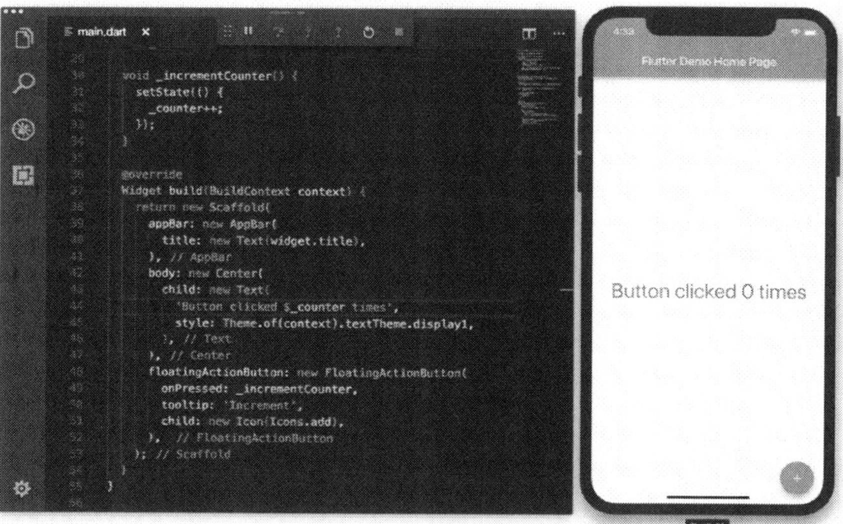

Improved Performance

Flutter was created with a high development rate in mind. Its stateful hot reload allows you to make changes to your code and witness it come to life in under a second without losing the app's state. Flutter also comes with a large number of widgets that may be customized, all of them are designed using the Modem Reactive Framework. Flutter promises to deliver 60 frames per second (fps) on devices with 120Hz updates, or 120 fps on devices with 120Hz updates. Frames must render every 16 milliseconds at 60 frames per second. Flutter code runs natively, which means its speed is impressive.

Free and Open

Flutter and Dart are both open-source and free to use, and they come with substantial documentation and community assistance to aid you with any problems you might run into. Flutter apps follow platform conventions and interface details such as scrolling, navigation, icons, fonts, and more. This is why apps built with Flutter feature on both the Apple AppStore and Google Play Store.

Fuchsia

Google's upcoming mobile operating system is called Fuchsia. Google is developing all of the apps for Fuchsia in Flutter. With its single codebase development and hot reload functionality for Android and iOS platforms, Flutter is noted for saving money. If developers are able to combine the dual strength of Flutter and Fuchsia in the future, they will be able to release apps on any platform, including smart homes, with minimal effort and in record time.

Flutter Source Code

Any collection of code, with or without comments, written in a human-readable programming language (usually as plain text) is referred to as **source code** in computer science. The source code of a program is specifically designed to aid the work of computer programmers, who write source code to outline the tasks that a computer should accomplish.

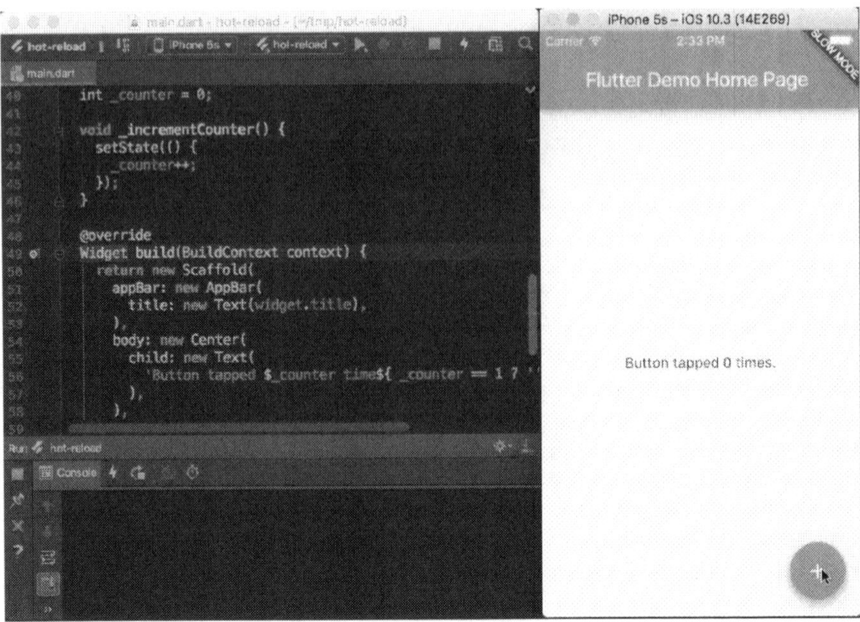

An assembler or compiler converts source code into binary machine code that can be executed by the computer. The machine code might then be saved and run at a later date. Alternatively, source code can be interpreted and run right away.

Flutter's source code is available in multiple places or repositories and is open source. Source code repositories are mostly used for backups and versioning, as well as for managing multiple source code versions and resolving conflicts that emerge from developers making overlapping modifications on multi-developer projects. For Flutter, this is hosted on GitHub here github.com/flutter/flutter and includes: the main repository, sample code repository, and plugins (which contains the source code for plugins developed by the core Flutter team to enable access to platform-specific APIs).

Flutter Framework

As far as framework goes, the major components of Flutter include:

- Dart platform
- Flutter engine
- Foundation library
- Design-specific widgets
- Flutter Development Tools (DevTools)

Dart Platform

In the last chapter, we discussed the Dart platform. Flutter apps are written in Dart and make extensive use of the language's advanced features. Flutter runs in the Dart virtual machine on Windows, macOS, and Linux, which has a just-in-time execution engine.

Flutter leverages just-in-time (JIT) compilation while building and debugging apps. This affords developers the opportunity to "hot reload," allowing changes to source files to be injected into a live application. Flutter adds support for stateful hot reload, which means that changes to source code are reflected in the running app without requiring a restart or losing state in most circumstances. Release versions of Flutter apps for Android and iOS are compiled with ahead-of-time (AOT) compilation for enhanced efficiency.

Flutter Engine

Flutter's engine, which is mostly built in C++, uses Google's Skia graphics package for low-level rendering. It is available on GitHub at github.com/flutter/engine and includes graphic rendering functionality as well as an interface (through the Flutter core libraries). The engine also works with platform-specific SDKs, such as those offered by Android and iOS.

The Flutter Engine is a portable runtime that may be used to host Flutter apps. It includes animation and graphics, file and network I/O, accessibility support, plugin architecture, and a Dart runtime and compile toolchain, among other things. Most developers interact with Flutter via the Flutter Framework, which provides a reactive framework and a set of platform, layout, and foundation widgets. More tooling may be obtained at github.com/flutter/engine/tree/master/lib/web_ui/dev#whats-felt if you want to run/contribute to the Flutter web engine. This is a program that was created to make web engine building easier.

Foundation Library

The lowest-level utility classes and functions utilized by all other levels of the Flutter framework are specified in this library. The Foundation library, written in Dart, provides basic classes and functions which are used to construct applications using Flutter, such as APIs to communicate with the engine. It can be easily accessed on GitHub through this link:

https://github.com/flutter/flutter/tree/master/packages/flutter/lib/src/foundation

Design-Specific Widgets

The Flutter framework has two sets of widgets that adhere to different design styles: Material Design widgets, which use Google's Material Design design language, and Cupertino widgets, which employ Apple's iOS Human Interface principles. The following are examples of available Flutter widgets:

- **AlertDialog:** Alerts are brief interruptions that need acknowledgement and inform the user of a problem. This component is implemented by the AlertDialog widget.
- **BottomNavigationBar:** Using bottom navigation bars, you can quickly explore and move between top-level views. This component is implemented by the BottomNavigationBar widget.
- **Checkboxes** allow the user to choose from a collection of many possibilities. This component is implemented by the Checkbox widget.
- **Drawer:** A Design panel that slides in from the Scaffold's edge to display navigation links in an application.
- **Expanded:** This is a widget that expands a Row, Column, or Flex's child.
- **Form:** A container that can be used to combine together several form field widgets (e.g. TextField widgets).
- **Gridview Widget:** A grid list is made up of a repetitive pattern of cells arranged vertically and horizontally. This component is implemented by the GridView widget.
- **IconButton:** An icon button is a picture that is printed on a Material widget and fills with color when it is touched (ink).
- **Image widget:** A widget that displays an image is known as an image widget.
- **ListBody:** A widget that arranges its children in a specific order along one axis, forcing them to the same dimension as the parent on the opposite axis.
- **MaterialApp:** This is a convenience widget that encapsulates a variety of widgets that are typically utilized in Material

Design applications. To learn more about Flutter widgets, visit flutter.dev/docs/reference/widgets.

Flutter Release Process

As far as release processes go, Flutter's is pretty straightforward. Google engineers work with the 'dev' branch while developing with Flutter on a daily basis. The 'dev' branch gets rolled into the 'beta' branch once a month. While the 'beta' branch is folded into the 'stable' branch every quarter. For more information, visit this link:

https://github.com/flutter/flutter/wiki/Release-process

Flutter Channels

"Flutter Channel" refers quite simply to a Flutter build release channel. Different release builds can be found in different channels, each with its own topicality and stability. As a result, Flutter channels allow a Flutter developer to select a version that is closer to the project's newest master build.

Another great thing about Flutter is that as a developer, you can choose which version of Flutter you prefer to use when working with it. For example, the 'stable' channel offers the developer a more 'stable' version of Flutter and so is where most people work. In this regard, the following channels are available:

Master

Master is the most up-to-date, cutting-edge build currently available. The master channel should only be used for development and should not be the foundation of your app. It's usually functional, but it's not always the best option. This is because no tests were conducted prior to the build; this channel may have broken functionality.

Dev

Dev is the latest fully-tested build as far as Flutter channels go. Usually functioning; however, see github.com/flutter/flutter/wiki/Bad-Builds for a list of all dev branch commits that should not be released to a more stable channel.

While you're at it, see github.com/flutter/flutter/wiki/Bad-Build-Identification for more information on how to spot bad dev builds to help you avoid pitfalls.

Beta

The beta channel, which is branched from master at the beginning of each month, comprises builds that are at most a month old and on average two weeks old. For over a month, this channel has had the same build, and cherrypick requests for repairs are welcomed. By the end of the month, the builds in this channel are generally more stable. The build enters the stable channel after around a quarter. You can find a list of changes since the last beta release at this link:

github.com/flutter/flutter/wiki/Changelog

Stable

Every quarter or so, fresh builds are added to the stable channel. This release comes from a branch of the beta channel that has had cherrypick requests for critical issues. This is the main channel that is approved for production use because there has been a stabilizing period in comparison to the beta channel. Aside from that, no other automated tests were carried out.

Which Channel To Use

This choice depends entirely on your peculiar use.

It is advisable to only utilize the stable channel if you're working on an app that will be released in a production environment.

The beta channel is a good place to go if your project is limited to features already in beta.

If you expect to encounter issues with that build, you might switch to the stable channel for improved functionality.

You might also wish to use the dev channel if you think two weeks to a month is too long, because the builds in this channel have passed automatic testing.

How to Change Channels

It's as simple as issuing a single command to change your current channel. The command's name is self-explanatory: **flutter channel**. The only required argument here is the channel name: stable, beta, dev, or master. You'll get a list of all available channels if you don't specify any arguments. You can see which channel you're on with the following command:

```
$ flutter channel

Flutter channels:

* stable

beta

dev

master
```

To switch channels, run **flutter channel [<channel-name>]**, and then run **flutter upgrade** to ensure you're on the latest. After selecting another channel, you should always use the following command to update the Flutter library: **flutter upgrade**. For further reading, visit:

github.com/flutter/flutter/wiki/Flutter-build-release-channels#how-to-change-channels.

Conclusion

Flutter is a fast, engaging, and modern method to deliver native apps if you're new to mobile. If you're a seasoned mobile developer, you can include Flutter into your existing process and tools to create new expressive user interfaces.

Flutter channels are a great way to try out new features ahead of time. You can participate in the development process by reporting any problems you have while testing the features before they are released to the stable channel. Take a look at the official documentation at this link for more details on the release process:

github.com/flutter/flutter/wiki/Release-process

FIVE

Installing Flutter 2.2

The goal of this chapter is to guide the reader through the process of installing Flutter 2.2 and an editor. Flutter 2.2 is based on Flutter 2, which expanded Flutter's capabilities beyond mobile to include web, desktop, and embedded applications.

It's made for a world of ambient computing, where users have a wide range of devices and form factors and want a consistent experience across all of them. With Flutter 2.2, businesses, tech firms, and innovators can create high-quality alternatives that reach the full potential of their target market, with the only limiting factor being creative inspiration (rather than target platform).

Developing on a PC for iOS

Flutter applications can be developed on a PC with no issues until you want to run your code on an Apple iOS device, such as an iPhone or iPad. Apple's XCode tool is the only reliable way to compile iOS applications on macOS. The good news is that Flutter is extremely cross-platform friendly, and you can complete 90% of the development on a PC, even if you plan to deploy to iOS. You can truly develop on one platform, run it on another, and trust that it will work almost flawlessly on both.

You'll have the option of buying, borrowing, or renting a Mac when it comes to testing and deployment. All you have to do now is use software like VMWare or Virtual Box to create a Mac virtual machine on your PC. You may also use a service like macincloud.com to rent a Mac in the cloud for about $20 per month.

Installing Flutter 2.2

I'm not going to go through every detail of Flutter installation, because there are lots of great places to learn about it. YouTube alone has numerous videos on the subject, and you can access all the information you need on flutter.io/docs/get-started/install, the official Flutter website.

Installation is not a particularly difficult procedure. I'll go over the basics, which are the same in all environments.

Prerequisites

Your development environment must meet the following basic requirements in order to install and execute Flutter:

- **Operating Systems:** x86-64 based, Windows 7 SP1 or later (64-bit).
- **Disk Space:** 1.64 GB (does not include IDE/tools disk space).
- Flutter also relies on the presence of Windows PowerShell 5.0, but the good news is that this is pre-installed with Windows 10.

Other needed command line tools you will need include:

- Bash
- Curl

- Mkdir
- Rm
- Unzip
- which

Software Needed

Git

Flutter installs and upgrades using Git. So, before you do anything else, make sure you have Git installed. In Git for Windows 2.x, you can use Git via the Windows Command Prompt option. Make sure you can run the **git** command straight from the command prompt (or PowerShell if you have the Windows version of Git installed). Installing Xcode, which includes Git, is recommended; however, Git can also be installed alone. Check out this link for more details:

git-scm.com/download/mac

Brew

On MacOS, the official approach to installing Flutter and its dependencies is a mixture of brew install, binary downloads, and reliance on system-installed ruby versions. If you're installing Flutter on a Mac, you need to first install Brew, as the Flutter Doctor will ask you to use Brew to install additional software as needed.

XCode Command Line Tools

If you are planning to install Flutter apps for iOS or on a Mac, you are definitely going to need to install the latest stable version of Xcode (from the web at developer.apple.com/xcode or from the Apple AppStore). Run this from the command line to configure the Xcode command line tools in order to use the newly installed version of Xcode:

```
$ sudo xcode-select --switch /Applications/Xcode.app/Contents/Developer

$ sudo xcodebuild -runFirstLaunch
```

When you want to use the most recent version of Xcode, this is the best approach to take. Open Xcode once and confirm, or execute **sudo xcodebuild -license** from the command line to ensure the Xcode license agreement is signed. If you need to use a different version, specify that path instead. It is not supported, and it is unlikely to work, to target bitcode with older versions of Xcode. Flutter apps can be executed on an iOS device or in the simulator using Xcode.

1. Download the Flutter SDK

We already explained how the Flutter SDK includes all of the tools you'll need to get started with Flutter programming. In addition to the Flutter Doctor, a really useful tool for setting up your Flutter Development environment,it also houses other Flutter SDK commands such as:

- **Flutter help:** Contains a set of flutter commands.
- **Flutter analyze:** Examines the Dart code in the project.
- Flutter Attach: Attach to a running application with Flutter.
- **Flutter bash-completion:** Setup scripts for command line shell completion.
- **Flutter build:** Builds commands for Flutter
- **Flutter channels:** Lists or switches flutter channels
- **Flutter clean:** Deletes the directories build/ and.dart tool/.
- **Flutter config:** Allows you to configure your flutter settings.
- **Flutter create:** Creates a new flutter project.
- **Flutter drive:** Runs Flutter driver tests for each present project.
- **Flutter emulators:** Generates, runs, and lists emulators.

Extract the file to a convenient location, such as:

```
$ cd ~/development
$ unzip ~/Downloads/flutter_macos_v1.12.13+hotfix.5-stable.zip
```

2. Set Up Your Path

The Flutter SDK includes command line utilities, such as Flutter Doctor, and these must be run from the command line. The Flutter SDK's **bin** subdirectory contains several command line tools. To run the command line tools from the command line, you must include the 'bin' folder (inside the flutter SDK) in your computer's path. Then, add the Flutter tool to your path as demonstrated below:

```
$ export PATH="$PATH:`pwd`/flutter/bin"
```

This command sets your **PATH** variable for the current terminal window only. As needed, the flutter tool also downloads platform-specific development binaries. iOS and Android binaries can be downloaded ahead of time in cases where pre-downloading these artifacts is preferred (for example, in hermetic build environments or with intermittent network access).

```
$ flutter precache
```

For additional download options, see **flutter help precache** command. To update your path:

- Identify the location where you placed the Flutter SDK.
- Open (or create) your shell's rc file. For example, macOS Mojave (and earlier) uses the Bash shell by default, so edit **$HOME/.bash_profile** or $**HOME/.bashrc**. macOS Catalina uses the Z shell by default, so edit **$HOME/.zshrc**. On your PC, the file path and filename will be different if you use a different shell.
- Include the following line and change **[PATH_TO_FLUTTER_GIT_DIRECTORY]** to be the path where you cloned Flutter's git repo:

```
$ export PATH="$PATH:[PATH_TO_FLUTTER_GIT_DIRECTORY]/flutter/bin"
```

- To refresh the current window, run **source $HOME/.rc file>**, or open a new terminal window to source the file automatically.
- Run the following command to see if the **flutter/bin** directory is now in your **PATH**:

```
$ echo $PATH
```

3. Run Flutter Doctor

This command examines your surroundings, diagnoses (as a doctor would) what's positive and negative about your Flutter development, and displays a report to your terminal window. It will also provide you with a summary and instructions for what you need to do to improve. To see if you need to install any dependencies to finish the setup, run the following command (with the **-v** flag to get more verbose output):

```
$ flutter doctor
```

The Dart SDK comes with Flutter, so you won't need to install it separately. Check the results for any additional applications you'll need to install or tasks you'll need to complete (shown in bold text). Consider the following example:

[-] Android toolchain - develop for Android devices

• Android SDK at /Users/obiwan/Library/Android/sdk

✗ Android SDK is missing command line tools; download from https://goo.gl/XxQghQ

• Try re-installing or updating your Android SDK,

visit https://flutter.dev/setup/#android-setup for detailed instructions.

Run the **flutter doctor** command again once you've installed any missing dependencies to make sure you've set everything up correctly.

4. Install Editor

After you've finished with the Flutter Doctor, you'll need to set up your editor. Flutter allows you to create apps with any text editor and your command line, but for a more seamless experience, one of the Flutter editor plugins is recommended. Code completion, syntax highlighting, widget editing assistance, run and debug support, and more are all available with these plugins.

Flutter's Android platform dependencies are supplied via a full installation of Android Studio. By the time you get through the Flutter Doctor, you should already have the Android Studio editor installed. This does not preclude you from using another editor; you can continue to use Visual Studio Code for the majority of your work while leaving Android Studio open.

Introduction: Android Studio

Android Studio is the official IDE for developing Android apps, offering a complete and well-supported (by Google) solution. Android Studio is a free program built on IntelliJ IDEA (and therefore fairly similar to IntelliJ in operation). It's a fantastic editor that works very well for designing Flutter iOS apps. Installing the Flutter plugins into Android Studio is the simplest method to get started with an editor.

To install Android Studio, follow these easy steps:

- Download and install Android Studio from developer. android.com/studio.
- Start Android Studio and follow the 'Android Studio Setup Wizard' instructions. The latest Android SDK, Android SDK Platform-Tools, and Android SDK Build-Tools will be automatically installed, and these are required by Flutter when working for Android.

Setting Up Your Android Device

- You'll need an Android device running Android 4.1 (API level 16) or higher to run and test your Flutter app.
- On your device, enable Developer settings and USB debugging. The manual has detailed instructions: developer.android.com/studio/debug/dev-options
- For Windows only: Install the Google USB Driver.
- Connect your phone to your computer with a USB cable. Allow your computer to access your device if prompted.
- Run the **flutter devices** command in the terminal to see if Flutter recognizes your connected Android device.

Setting Up the Android Emulator

Follow these steps to get your Flutter app ready to launch and test on the Android emulator.

- On your machine, enable VM acceleration.
- Select **Create Virtual Device** in **Android Studio → Tools → Android → AVD Manager**. (The Android submenu appears only when you're working on an Android project.)
- Select **Next** after selecting a device definition.
- Select **Next** after selecting one or more system images for the Android versions you want to imitate. It's best to use an x86 or x86 64 image.
- To activate hardware acceleration, go to Emulated Performance and select **Hardware → GLES 2.0**.
- Select **Finish** after double-checking the AVD configuration.
- In the toolbar of Android Virtual Device Manager, select **Run**.When the emulator starts up, it displays the default canvas for the OS version and device you've chosen.

Installing Flutter and Dart Plugins

- To begin, open Android Studio.
- Open Plugin Preferences (on macOS, **Preferences → Plugins**, on Windows, **File → Settings → Plugins**).
- Select **Marketplace**, then **Flutter** from the drop-down menu.
- When prompted to install the Dart plugin, select **Yes**.
- When prompted, select **Restart**.

If you already use Intellij, you can simply install the Flutter plugin in the same way, as it is in Android Studio (see above).

Flutter Outline

The Flutter Outline is one of the best features of the Android Studio. When you edit a file, it displays the Widgets defined in that file, along with their variables, code, and structure. It also allows you to add Centering, Padding, Rows, Columns, and other features to Widgets in your 'build' methods.

Visual Studio Code

Visual Studio Code is an excellent alternative to Android Studio, and it is a little more lightweight (runs faster, uses less memory). It's a terrific editor that's both quick and free to use. If Visual Studio Code is your preferred editor, follow these steps to install the Flutter and Dart plugins.

1. Start Visual Studio Code.
2. Select **View → Command Palette** from the menu.
3. Select **Extensions: install** after typing "install." Extensions should be installed.
4. In the extensions search window, type "flutter," choose **Flutter** from the list, and click **Install**. This also installs the Dart plugin, which is essential.

For further reading, visit:

flutter.io/docs/get-started/editor?tab=vscode

Mac Platform Setup

Flutter apps for iOS, Android, and the web are supported on macOS (technical preview release). To build and execute your first Flutter app, complete the platform setup processes in the steps below.

Set Up an iOS Simulator

Locate the Simulator on your Mac using Spotlight or the following command:

```
$ open -a Simulator
```

Check the settings in the simulator's **Hardware → Device** menu to make sure your simulator is running on a 64-bit device (iPhone 5s or later).

Simulated high-screen-density iOS devices may overflow your screen depending on the screen size of your development machine. In the simulator, go to **Window → Scale** and adjust the device scale. That's all there is for installing Flutter on a Mac using Xcode.

Activate Desktop Support

To activate Win32 desktop support, type the following in the command prompt:

```
$ flutter config --enable-windows-desktop
```

To enable Windows UWP desktop support, move to the dev channel, upgrade Flutter, then enable UWP with the commands below.

```
$ flutter channel dev

$ flutter upgrade

$ flutter config --enable-windows-uwp-desktop
```

For more information, visit https://flutter.dev/desktop.

Finally, use the Flutter Doctor to validate your setup through these last steps:

- Select **View → Command Palette** from the menu bar.
- Type "doctor" and select **Flutter: Run Flutter Doctor**.
- In the OUTPUT window, review carefully for any problems. Make sure Flutter is selected from the dropdown menus in the various Output Options.

Conclusion

Flutter 2.2 is the best version of Flutter yet. Its updates make it easier for developers to monetize their apps through in-app purchases while staying connected to cloud services and APIs. Its tooling and language features also come in handy for the elimination of a whole class of errors, improvement of app performance, and reduction of package size. Dart is updated in this release as well. Support for type aliases is also included, to improve readability and provide a better approach for some refactoring circumstances. To learn more, visit:

flutter.dev/docs/get-started/install

SIX

Flutter Project 1 - Build Your First App

Flutter's popularity is growing so much daily that most people will recommend Flutter for creating a hybrid app. If you're a developer, you've probably heard someone ask (or asked yourself), "What are some authentic Flutter projects I can work on to obtain real-world experience?" Well, the goal of this chapter is to provide you with concrete examples and the step-by-step instructions you'll need to build some interesting Flutter projects from the ground up.

1. Creating Your Flutter Project

Follow the steps outlined in the previous chapter to install Andoird Studio if you have not already done so. Now open Android Studio and select **New Flutter project** from the menu.

Click **File → New → New Flutter Project** if you're already in the project.

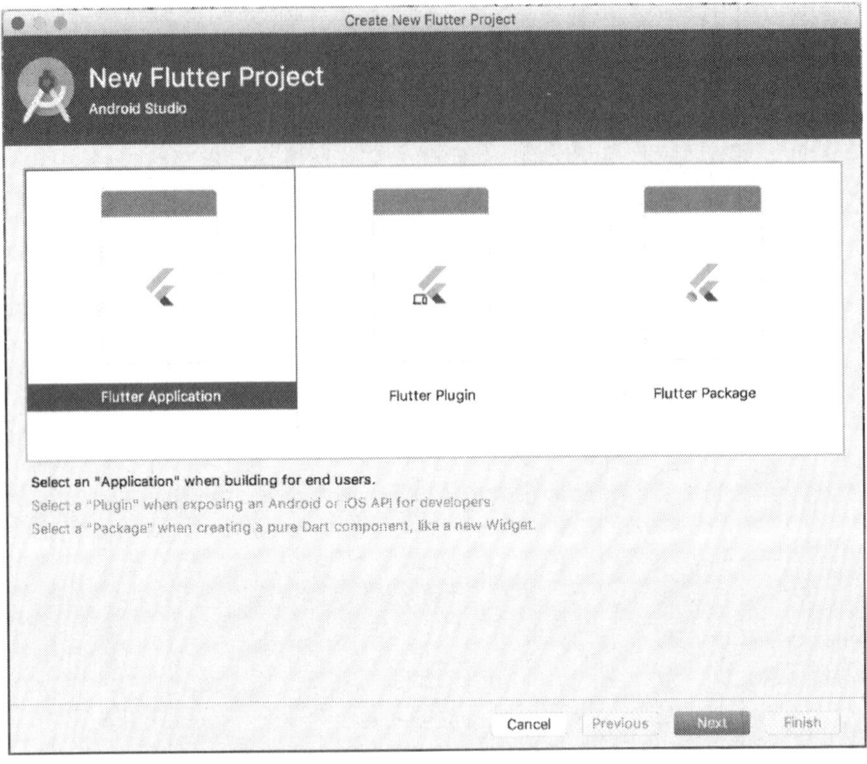

We're going to make a Flutter Application, which is a full-featured iOS/Android app. As you're learned, plugins and packages are components designed to enhance and add functionality to a Flutter project or to make routine chores easier, e.g. barcode scanners or wrappers for Firebase services. All packages are listed on pub.dartlang.org. To continue, click **Next**.

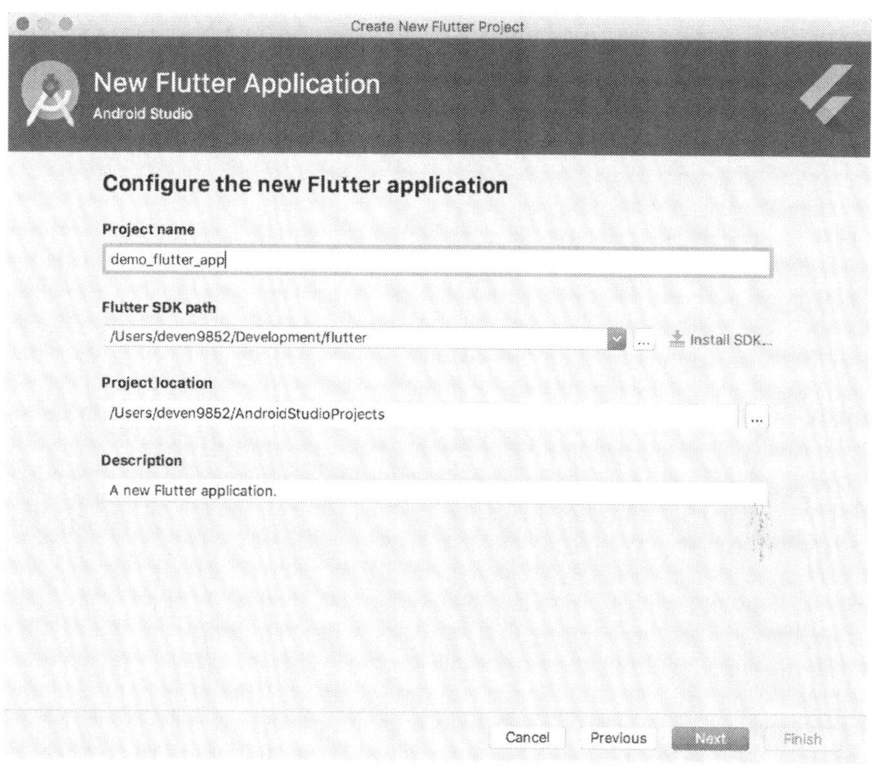

At this point, feel free to give your project a name. For our purposes, I'll just name this project **demo_flutter_app**. If you encounter any problems at this stage, it could either mean that there is a problem with the SDK path or that your Flutter app was not installed correctly. Retrace your steps and correct any errors. Then click **Next** to continue.

2. Set The Package Name

An Android app's package name identifies it on the device, in the Google Play Store, and in compatible third-party Android shops. It's a one-of-a-kind name used to distinguish your app from others on the Play Store, and isn't accessible to the public. It is normally made up of three components, but it can also be made up of two. Mozilla's Firefox Browser for Android, for example, has the package ID **org.mozilla.-firefox**.

The **company_domain + app_name** typically makes up the package name, but for this sample project, simply **example.com** would suffice.

A word of note: If you want to upload your app to the Google Play Store, avoid using example.com, because it is restricted.

For platform-specific tasks, the last two options allow you to use native Kotlin or Swift code. For the time being, you can ignore this section. To complete this stage of the project, click **Finish** as shown below:

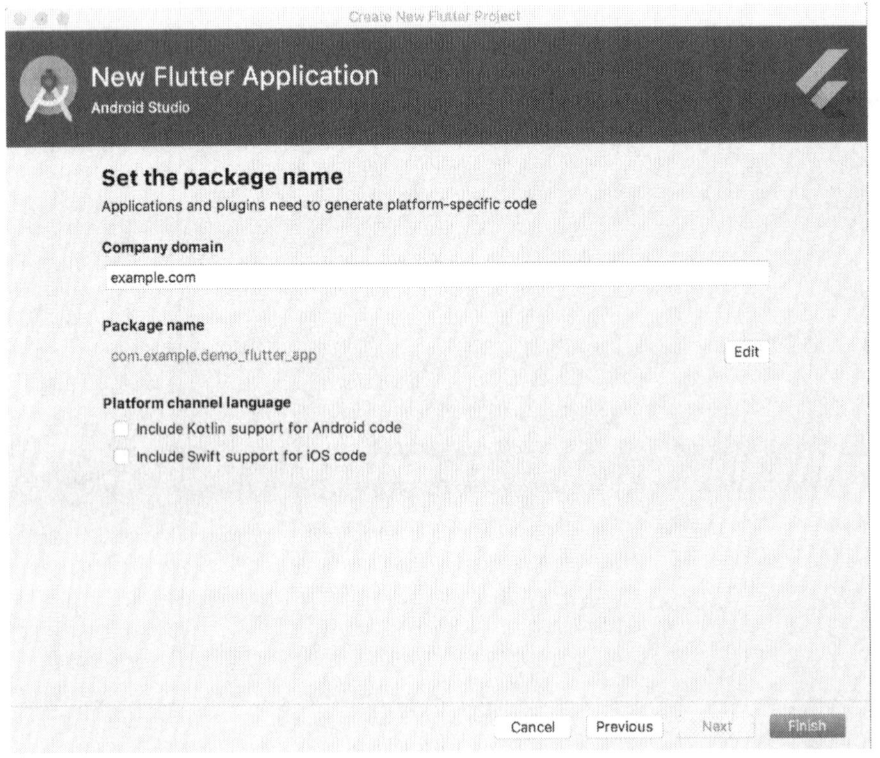

3. Exploring the Project

On the right side of your screen, you should be looking at some code right about now, while on the left, you're probably seeing some files. If you're new to mobile programming, the code may appear strange—but before we get into the code, let's get a better understanding of the project's files. To build a basic app with flutter, you only need to focus on the **lib** directory and the **pubspec.yaml** file.

The **lib** directory has all of the primary Dart code for running your app, while the **pubspec.yaml** file contains all of the packages you've imported. (For Android developers, this is the equivalent of adding dependencies to your gradle files.) In traditional Android development, separate layout and Java/Kotlin files are required, but Flutter eliminates this requirement entirely.

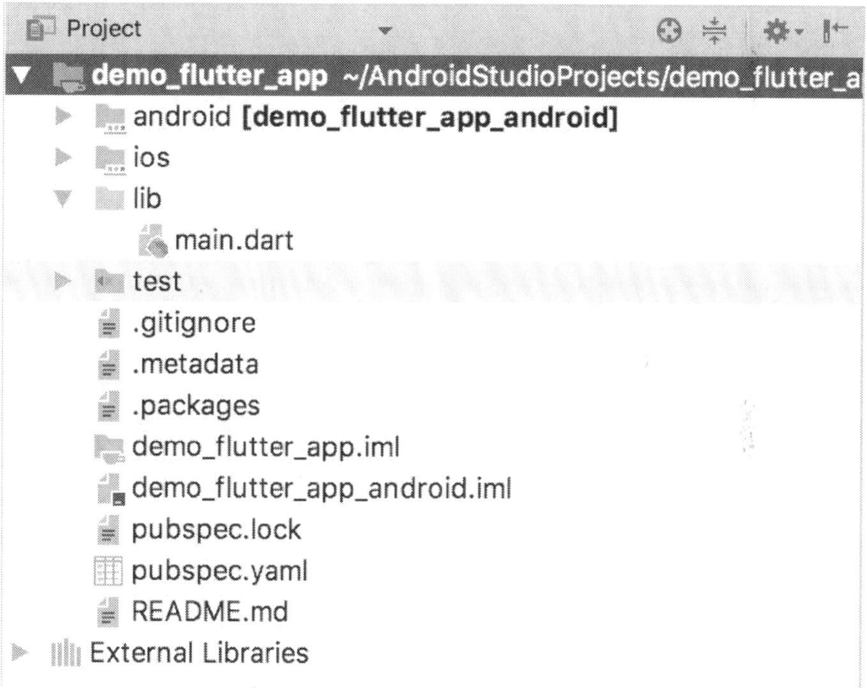

The **test** directory is for writing Dart tests that are analogous to Espresso-based instrumented tests in Android. The tests are important because they allow you to verify that a component works without having to perform the task yourself. A sample test has been developed for you, which you can run to see how it works.

Let's move on to the codes on the left side of your screen.

4. Understanding the Default App and Code

Flutter produces a default counter app for you when you create the project. The app merely keeps track of how many times the button is pressed.

Have a look at the **main.dart** file. This is the app's default landing page. Before we go into the codes, we must first grasp a basic idea in Flutter: a Widget.

So, what exactly is a widget? A widget is any component of an interface that allows a user to utilize your app to execute a function or access a service. Every visible element, layout, and even the app itself are widgets in Flutter. This is similar to an Android View, but Flutter takes it a step further. A widget is any visible element or structure, such as an image, text, or layout. These widgets are used to construct our screen. Let's have a look at how it's done in the default app.

```
import 'package:flutter/material.dart';

void main() => runApp(new MyApp());

class MyApp extends StatelessWidget {

@override

Widget build(BuildContext context) {

return new MaterialApp(

title: 'Flutter Demo',

theme: new ThemeData(

primarySwatch: Colors.blue,
```

```
),
home: new MyHomePage(title: 'Flutter Demo Home Page'),
);
}
}
class MyHomePage extends StatefulWidget {
MyHomePage({Key key, this.title}) : super(key: key);
final String title;
@override
_MyHomePageState createState() => new _MyHomePageState();
}
class _MyHomePageState extends State<MyHomePage> {
int _counter = 0;
void _incrementCounter() {
setState(() {
_counter++;
});
}
@override
Widget build(BuildContext context) {
return new Scaffold(
```

```
appBar: new AppBar(
title: new Text(widget.title),
),
body: new Center(
child: new Column(
mainAxisAlignment: MainAxisAlignment.center,
children: <Widget>[
new Text(
'You have pushed the button this many times:',
),
new Text(
'$_counter',
style: Theme.of(context).textTheme.display1,
),
],
),
),
floatingActionButton: new FloatingActionButton(
onPressed: _incrementCounter,
tooltip: 'Increment',
child: new Icon(Icons.add),
),
);
```

```
}
}
```

I've tried to keep things basic by removing some comments, but this is essentially the project's default code. While this appears to be a lot for a default project, keep in mind that this is your *complete* project. Try to read the comments I've left out if you can. This page does not have its own layout file. Let's have a look at the most significant elements of the code.

The main function is the first thing you see, and it just launches a new instance of the program. The notation **=>** creates a new app. For a more in-depth understanding of Dart notation and syntactic sugar, I recommend taking their language tour.

There's also the app itself, dubbed MyApp, which extends a stateless widget. Widgets are divided into two categories; **stateful widgets** and **stateless widgets**. To explain their differences plainly, if a page is static and contains only static information, it should be made into a stateless widget. Make a stateful widget out of anything on a page that needs to update. The main app is a stateless widget in and of itself. The same is true for pages within the app.

The **build** function creates the widgets from scratch. Consider this to be the construction of the layout. We return a MaterialApp from the MyApp class, which is a widget that builds a Material App. The title, theme, and homepage are all set in the MaterialApp. If you alter the **home:** argument, the app's first opening page will change, as well. The Flutter team created these widgets to help you avoid writing a lot of boilerplate code.

```
return new MaterialApp(
```

```
title: 'Flutter Demo',
theme: new ThemeData(
primarySwatch: Colors.blue,
),
home: new MyHomePage(title: 'Flutter Demo Home Page'),
);
```

Now that the app has been developed, let's look at the **MyHomePage** class, which is the app's first page. The primary distinction is that this page is a stateful widget. When a button is hit, we want to *alter something dynamically* on the website—in this case, the counter text.

The term "state" simply refers to the current state of a page, which keeps all the dynamic elements on the page, such as text submitted in a text field or the number of clicks for a counter. That's why the state has a **counter** field that stores the count.

We really build the page we see with numerous other widgets in the **build** method of the **MyHomePageState** class. For instance, a Scaffold is a widget that makes adding things like AppBars (ActionBars), Bottom Navigation, and Drawers much easier. An AppBar, a floating action button, and a body are included in the default code.

The body has a Center widget that simply centers everything on the screen within it. A Column is placed inside the main widget. A Column is a vertical, linear grouping of items (similar to Android's LinearLayout).

```
new Column(
```

```
mainAxisAlignment: MainAxisAlignment.center,
children: <Widget>[
new Text(
'You have pushed the button this many times:',
),
new Text(
'$_counter',
style: Theme.of(context).textTheme.display1,
),
],
),
```

A Column has a **children** element, in which all of your vertically organized items are placed. There is some text for the counter itself inside our Column.

This concludes the app's design. We'll look at how the app updates once it's been executed.

Note that a **child** parameter merely specifies what is contained within a widget. A floating action button with a child as an icon is just a button with an icon inside it.

5. Running the App

To run the app, you must first launch an emulator. To launch an emulator, choose one from the list of emulators dropdown menu. Click the **Run** button after the emulator has started.

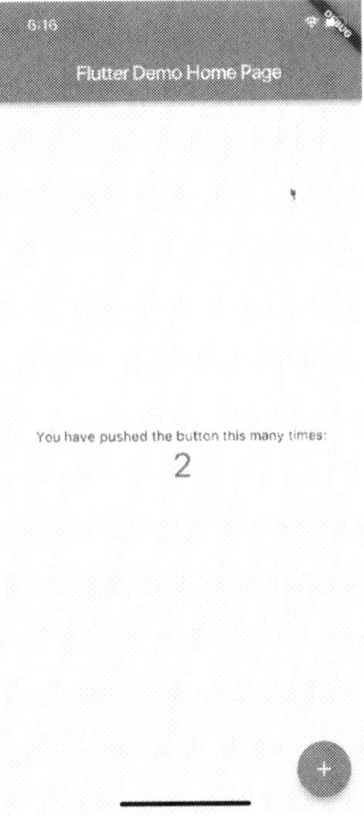

This is the app that appears. The count is increased by clicking the Fl**oatingActionButton**. Let's take a closer look at how that happens.

```
floatingActionButton: new FloatingActionButton(

onPressed: _incrementCounter,

tooltip: 'Increment',

child: new Icon(Icons.add),

),
```

The **onTap** parameter of the **FloatingActionButton** launches a function named **_incrementCounter()**.

```
void _incrementCounter() {

setState(() {

_counter++;

});

}
```

The increment itself is rather simple. The number of taps is stored in a variable called **_counter**. For its part, **setState()** is a function that tells the app that it needs to refresh the page. As a result, without **setState()**, the counter variable would increase, while the text remained unchanged. **setState()** causes the entire page to be refreshed.

This was a lot of information to take in, and it's fine if you need to read it again to fully get it. To see how things operate, try adjusting a few values.

For Android developers, notice how this method eliminates the requirement for view IDs entirely. This is because, unlike Java/Kotlin development, the text in a field cannot be fetched at any time from the view itself—and so any modification must be saved in a variable.

Flutter may appear difficult at first, since it is a significant departure from traditional Android/iOS app development. The good news is that it automates a number of issues that previously plagued developers. After becoming accustomed to this style of app development, the old method appears laborious.

To fully comprehend all aspects of this chapter, you may need to read it several times. We'll look at additional Flutter projects in the following chapters to aid your comprehension.

SEVEN

Flutter Project 2 - Build a Song App

We'll take a closer look at Flutter Development on the Android Platform in this chapter, but keep in mind that you'll require Android Studio for Android and XCode for iOS. So, before you begin the app development process, make sure you have Android Studio, Flutter, and Dart plugins installed. If you haven't already done so, please refer to the earlier chapters of this book for help.

Music is an emotional language, and basic song apps have been a clear need in recent years. Users listen to their favorite songs in order to reduce stress, improve their creative abilities, and more. You will inevitably create a song app in your career as a developer, so consider this chapter practice.

In this chapter, you will learn:

- How to integrate a music player into your flutter app in this chapter.
- How to get music from external storage and play it from an assets file.
- How to use a URL to play music (internet).

- How to control your music player's volume and how to pause and play a song.

1. Packages To Be Used

A **package** is a namespace that holds a collection of classes, interfaces, and sub-packages that are all of the same kind. Flutter always supports shared packages, which are provided to the Flutter and Dart ecosystem by other developers. For this project, we will use two major packages: the **flutter_audio_query** and **audio_manager** packages.

flutter_audio_query Package

To get the music from our external storage (e.g. mobile phone or memory card), we'll utilize the flutter_audio_query package. You can check it out at pub.dev/packages/flutter_audio_query.

audio_manager Package

For its part, the **audio_manager** package will supply us with a number of methods and functions to use in our app, such as play, pause, seek, and increase or decrease volume. This can be accessed at pub.dev/packages/audio_manager.

You can see the demo of our proposed app below:

2. Setting Up the Project

To do this properly, you'll need to import the packages as illustrated below:

```
import 'package:flutter_audio_query/flutter_audio_query.dart';

import 'package:audio_manager/audio_manager.dart';
```

Implement alterations to your **AndroidManifest.xml** file.

```
<application
...
android:usesCleartextTraffic="true"
...
>
```

Similarly, modify your **build.gradle** file.

```
defaultConfig {
minSdkVersion 23
}
```

3. Playing Music Using Internet and Assets

Start by creating an audio manager instance as shown below:

```
var audioManagerInstance = AudioManager.instance;
```

Playing Music Using the Start Method

To play music, we can use the **start()** function provided by AudioManager. A URL, title, description, cover, and auto are all required.

```
onTap: () {
audioManagerInstance
.start("song URL", "song title",
desc: "description",
auto: true,
cover: "cover URL")
.then((err) {
print(err);
});
},
```

To play music from an assets file, simply update the song URL to the assets file path:

```
onTap: () {
audioManagerInstance
.start("assets/music.mp3"song title",
desc: "description",
```

```
auto: true,

cover: "assets/cover.png")

.then((err) {

print(err);

});

},
```

---

4. Getting Music Files from Our External Storage

We'll use **FutureBuilder** to get the music files from the external storage, because **FlutterAudioQuery** returns a **future**. **GetSongs**, **getSongsFromArtist**, **getSongsFromAlbum**, **getSongsFromArtistAlbum**, and more methods are available in this class.

In this example, I'll simply utilize the **getSongs** method to keep the logic clean and basic. You are free to use as many as you like.

```
FutureBuilder(

future: FlutterAudioQuery()

.getSongs(sortType: SongSortType.RECENT_YEAR),

builder: (context, snapshot) {

List<SongInfo> songInfo = snapshot.data;

if (snapshot.hasData) return SongWidget(songList: songInfo);

return Container(

height: MediaQuery.of(context).size.height * 0.4,

child: Center(
```

```
child: Row(
mainAxisAlignment: MainAxisAlignment.center,
children: <Widget>[
CircularProgressIndicator(),
SizedBox(
width: 20,
),
Text(
"Loading....",
style: TextStyle(fontWeight: FontWeight.bold),
)
],
),
),
);
},
)
```

SongWidget

We need a path of a song to be able to play the music from external memory. The **filePath** field of the **SongInfo** class is used to obtain the path of the music file.

```
onTap: () {
audioManagerInstance
.start("file://${song.filePath}", song.title,
desc: song.displayName,
auto: true,
cover: song.albumArtwork)
.then((err) {
print(err);
});
},
```

Also, assess the raw SongWidget Dart hosted by Github at this link:

gist.github.com/anmolseth06/
11a33c09b1b4f085494835b1b55bb263#file-songwidget-dart

5. Setting Up the Audio

This is the most important part, because this controls various audio events.

```
void setupAudio() {
audioManagerInstance.onEvents((events, args) {
switch (events) {
```

```
case AudioManagerEvents.start:
_slider = 0;
break;
case AudioManagerEvents.seekComplete:
_slider = audioManagerInstance.position.inMilliseconds /
audioManagerInstance.duration.inMilliseconds;
setState(() {});
break;
case AudioManagerEvents.playstatus:
isPlaying = audioManagerInstance.isPlaying;
setState(() {});
break;
case AudioManagerEvents.timeupdate:
_slider = audioManagerInstance.position.inMilliseconds /
audioManagerInstance.duration.inMilliseconds;
audioManagerInstance.updateLrc(args["position"].toString());
setState(() {});
break;
case AudioManagerEvents.ended:
audioManagerInstance.next();
setState(() {});
break;
default:
```

```
break;
}
});
}
```

To initialize your Audio setup, take the steps below.

```
void initState() {
super.initState();
setupAudio();
}
```

6. Creating a Control Panel

Everything in a Flutter app is a widget, which is an application in and of itself. Widgets with changeable and immutable conditions, for example, are classified as stateless or stateful respectively.

The scaffold widget is a screen component architecture that comprises all of the common screen elements. With an app bar, body, menu, and other components, hierarchy can be a tough task. Flutter's widget saves you a lot of time and work when it comes to app creation, but it does require you to learn how to create a Widget. Other widgets should be included in the Widget.

Stateless widgets are immutable, which implies that none of their properties can be modified and that all of their values are set in stone.

Stateful widgets, on the other hand, are in such states that may change over the widget's lifespan. The **StatefulWidget** class can be deleted and recreated, but the **State** class persists throughout the widget's lifespan. Considering that everything on the screen in Flutter is a Widget, it makes sense for our ControlPanel to be a Widget as well—and a StatefulWidget at that. This is because the ControlPanel communicates with the device and so must know everything about it, including internal data, functions, and connection state.

This Widget is designed to keep track of and modify anything that cannot be accessed directly from the main page (as they are now in two separate modules), and as such, the control panel must have its own state, a copy of the required data. This panel has a play/pause button, previous button, next button, and a songProgress Slider:

```
Widget bottomPanel() {
return Column(children: <Widget>[
Padding(
padding: EdgeInsets.symmetric(horizontal: 16),
child: songProgress(context),
),
Container(
padding: EdgeInsets.symmetric(vertical: 16),
child: Row(
mainAxisAlignment: MainAxisAlignment.spaceEvenly,
children: <Widget>[
CircleAvatar(
```

```
child: Center(
child: IconButton(
icon: Icon(
Icons.skip_previous,
color: Colors.white,
),
onPressed: () => audioManagerInstance.previous()),
),
backgroundColor: Colors.cyan.withOpacity(0.3),
),
CircleAvatar(
radius: 30,
child: Center(
child: IconButton(
onPressed: () async {
if(audioManagerInstance.isPlaying)
audioManagerInstance.toPause();
audioManagerInstance.playOrPause();
},
padding: const EdgeInsets.all(0.0),
icon: Icon(
audioManagerInstance.isPlaying
? Icons.pause
: Icons.play_arrow,
```

```
color: Colors.white,
),
),
),
),
CircleAvatar(
backgroundColor: Colors.cyan.withOpacity(0.3),
child: Center(
child: IconButton(
icon: Icon(
Icons.skip_next,
color: Colors.white,
),
onPressed: () => audioManagerInstance.next()),
),
),
],
),
),
]);
}
```

---

7. SongDuration

This function is used to format the song's duration in milliseconds, but we'll convert it into the more useful format 00:00. The format is a string 00:00 in this case. It returns — : — if the duration is nil; otherwise, it returns the duration in the supplied format.

```
String _formatDuration(Duration d) {

if (d == null) return "--:--";

int minute = d.inMinutes;

int second = (d.inSeconds > 60) ? (d.inSeconds % 60) :
d.inSeconds;

String format = ((minute < 10) ? "0$minute" : "$minute") +

":" +

((second < 10) ? "0$second" : "$second");

return format;

}
```

---

8. SongProgress

This is simply a widget that displays the progress of your audio or video player. This widget connects to a media player more easily than the Flutter Slider widget. It can also display the buffered status of streamed media.

```
Widget songProgress(BuildContext context) {

var style = TextStyle(color: Colors.black);
```

```
return Row(
children: <Widget>[
Text(
_formatDuration(audioManagerInstance.position),
style: style,
),
Expanded(
child: Padding(
padding: EdgeInsets.symmetric(horizontal: 5),
child: SliderTheme(
data: SliderTheme.of(context).copyWith(
trackHeight: 2,
thumbColor: Colors.blueAccent,
overlayColor: Colors.blue,
thumbShape: RoundSliderThumbShape(
disabledThumbRadius: 5,
enabledThumbRadius: 5,
),
overlayShape: RoundSliderOverlayShape(
overlayRadius: 10,
),
activeTrackColor: Colors.blueAccent,
inactiveTrackColor: Colors.grey,
),
```

```
child: Slider(
value: _slider ?? 0,
onChanged: (value) {
setState(() {
_slider = value;
});
},
onChangeEnd: (value) {
if (audioManagerInstance.duration != null) {
Duration msec = Duration(
milliseconds:
(audioManagerInstance.duration.inMilliseconds *
value)
.round());
audioManagerInstance.seekTo(msec);
}
},
)),
),
),
Text(
_formatDuration(audioManagerInstance.duration),
style: style,
),
```

```
],
);
}
```

Conclusion

In comparison to prior extensive coding sessions, designing simple apps with Flutter 2 takes only a few minutes. You come up with a feature, implement it, and move on to the next. In the next chapters, we will build on more projects with Flutter to further demonstrate this.

EIGHT

Flutter Project 3 - Build a Login UI

The **user interface (UI)** is the set of screens, pages, and visual elements—such as buttons and icons—that allow a person to engage with a product or service at its most basic level. In this chapter, we'll use the Flutter SDK to create a lovely Login UI.

Prerequisites

This project requires a basic understanding of Flutter and Dart. Fortunately, we went over this in great detail in the previous chapters of this book. Knowledge of JavaScript, particularly ES6 features, will be beneficial.

- If you haven't already, you should install the Visual Studio Code editor on your computer. We'll use VSC for this project, because we've already used the Audio Studio Code editor. It can be obtained here: code.visualstudio.com/Download
- The Flutter plugin for Visual Studio Code also needs to be downloaded and installed. Chapter 5 contains instructions for this, and more information can be found at flutter.io/docs/get-started/editor?tab=vscode.

Project Setup

We'll mostly concentrate on developing our app here. If you need to, look at flutter.io/docs/get-started/install for further information on setting up your environment properly. This site is quite useful and will walk you through installing Flutter SDK on your PC (if you haven't already) and your operating system.

To create a new project, press **ctrl+shift+p** or **cmd+shift+p** in your code editor and name it. You could also simply run **flutter create your_project_name**. After that, you'll have a brand-new Flutter project.

Directory Structure

Drag the project into Visual Studio Code once it's been created. We're adopting Visual Studio Code because it provides great Flutter support, including Dart syntax, code completion, and debugging tools (which we'll explore in depth later). You should see the following directory structure by default:

- **android**: This folder contains Android-related files. If you've ever worked on a cross-platform mobile app, this, along with the ios folder, should be rather familiar.
- **ios**: The location of iOS-related files.
- **lib**: This is where you'll spend the most of your time. It includes a **main.dart** file by default, which is the Flutter app's entry point.
- **test**: This is where you'll place the app's unit testing code. In this chapter, we won't be working on this.
- **pubspec.yaml**: this file specifies your app's version and build number. It's also the directory where your dependencies are defined.

There are several more folders and files in this directory, but they aren't necessary for the purposes of this chapter, and you won't need them most of the time.

1. Definition of Assets

Both code and assets can be included in Flutter apps (sometimes called resources). A file that is bundled and published with your program, which is available at runtime, is referred to as an **asset**. Static data (for example, JSON files), configuration files, icons, and images (JPEG, WebP, GIF, animated WebP/GIF, PNG, BMP, and WBMP) are all common types of assets.

To identify assets required by an app, Flutter uses the **pubspec.yaml** file, which is located at the root of your project. To define your assets, navigate to the p**ubspec.yaml** file and make the following changes:

```
//../pubspec.yaml

name: flutter_login_ui

description: A new Flutter project.

# The following defines the version and build number for your application.

# A version number is three numbers separated by dots, like 1.2.43

# followed by an optional build number separated by a +.

# Both the version and the builder number may be overridden in flutter

# build by specifying --build-name and --build-number, respectively.

# Read more about versioning at semver.org.
```

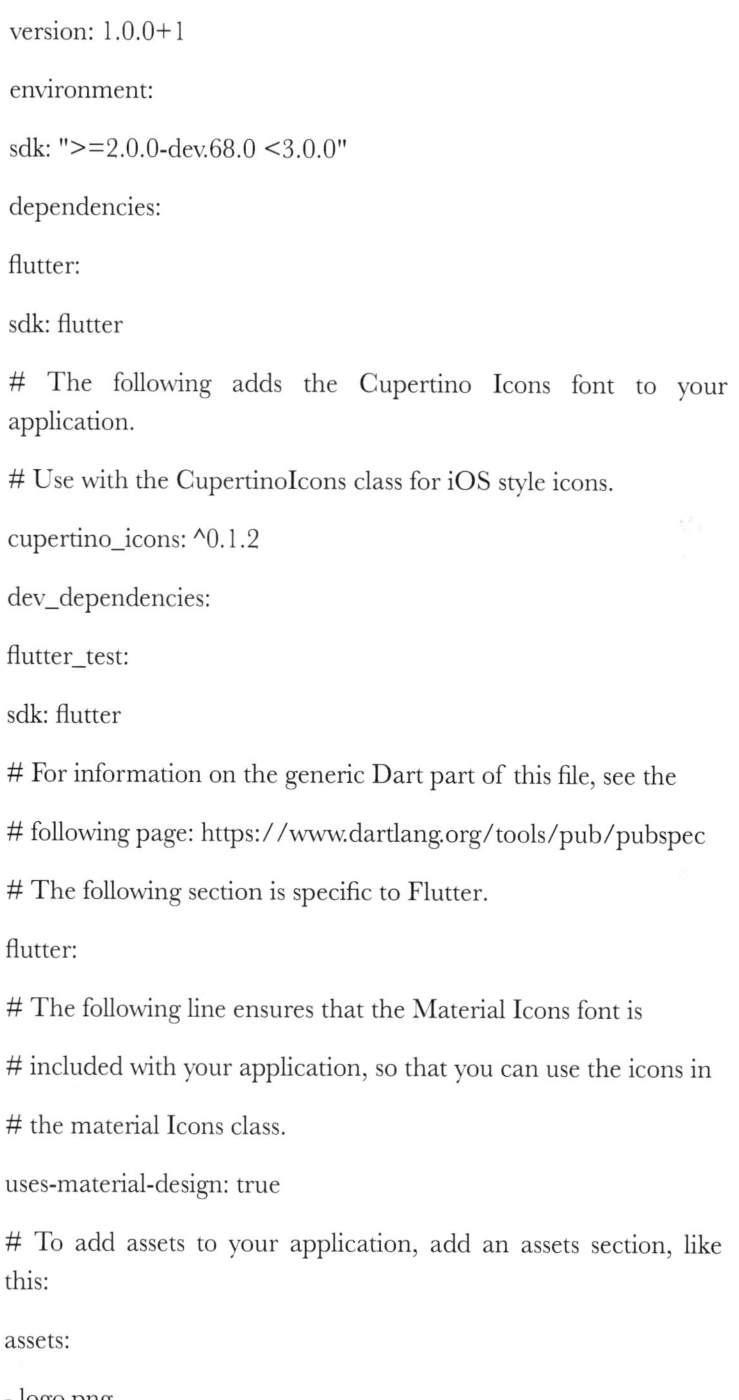

```
version: 1.0.0+1

environment:

sdk: ">=2.0.0-dev.68.0 <3.0.0"

dependencies:

flutter:

sdk: flutter

# The following adds the Cupertino Icons font to your application.

# Use with the CupertinoIcons class for iOS style icons.

cupertino_icons: ^0.1.2

dev_dependencies:

flutter_test:

sdk: flutter

# For information on the generic Dart part of this file, see the

# following page: https://www.dartlang.org/tools/pub/pubspec

# The following section is specific to Flutter.

flutter:

# The following line ensures that the Material Icons font is

# included with your application, so that you can use the icons in

# the material Icons class.

uses-material-design: true

# To add assets to your application, add an assets section, like this:

assets:

- logo.png
```

```
fonts:

- family: Montserrat

fonts:

- asset: fonts/Montserrat-Regular.ttf
```

In the root of your Flutter project, create assets and fonts directories. Their assets and fonts are available at github.com/Ethiel97/flutter login **ui/tree/master/assets** and github.com/Ethiel97/flutter login **ui/tree/master/fonts**, respectively. We uploaded a **logo.png** and the **Montserrat-Regular.ttf** font to our **../assets** and **../fonts** folders, respectively. We'll use these assets in our app later on in the project.

2. Build the UI

Building our UI starts from the **..lib/main.dart** file. We begin by importing the Material library from Flutter as shown below:

```
import 'package:flutter/material.dart';
```

The **MaterialApp**, **Scaffold**, and **AppBar** widgets that we use in our app are included in this package. The methods we're utilizing are either from a library you've imported or are built into the Flutter framework. After that, move on to the line that says:

```
void main() => runApp(MyApp())
```

As this is our program's entrance point, it must always be defined if you want to render anything on the screen. If you're familiar with JavaScript ES6 features, you'll recognize the **fat-arrow (=>)**. We're actually running the **runApp() function** inside the **main() method** because it's a more compact way of declaring functions. The **MyApp widget** is made the root of the widget tree with this function. The widget, along with its descendants, is effectively rendered into the screen.

Remember that with Flutter, practically everything is a widget, and each one can have its own set of properties and child widgets. The two primary types of widgets have been discussed in previous chapters: these are the **stateful** and **stateless** widgets. The former manages its own internal state and keeps track of it, while the latter doesn't and is prone to change.

The **MyApp widget** is the next thing we need to define at this point. To do so, make the following changes to your **MyApp class**, changing only the title property:

```
class MyApp extends StatelessWidget {

// This widget is the root of your application.

@override

Widget build(BuildContext context) {

return MaterialApp(

title: 'Flutter login UI',

theme: ThemeData(

// This is the theme of your application.

//

// Try running your application with "flutter run". You'll see the

// application has a blue toolbar. Then, without quitting the
app, try
```

```
// changing the primarySwatch below to Colors.green and then invoke
// "hot reload" (press "r" in the console where you ran "flutter run",
// or simply save your changes to "hot reload" in a Flutter IDE).
// Notice that the counter didn't reset back to zero; the application
// is not restarted.
primarySwatch: Colors.blue,
),
home: MyHomePage(title: 'Flutter Login'),
);
}
}
```

The code above creates a new **MaterialApp widget** with the title, theme, and home page of our app. It's a stateless widget, and to create this, all you need to do add the following code to the **StatelessWidget class**:

```
class MyApp extends StatelessWidget {
// ...
}
```

Next, we'll define our **home widget**, which will be a stateful widget this time—meaning it will include fields that can affect how it appears. There is no need for you to make any alterations here:

```
class MyHomePage extends StatefulWidget {

MyHomePage({Key key, this.title}) : super(key: key);

// This widget is the home page of your application. It is stateful, meaning

// that it has a State object (defined below) that contains fields that affect

// how it looks.

// This class is the configuration for the state. It holds the values (in this

// case the title) provided by the parent (in this case the App widget) and

// used by the build method of the State. Fields in a Widget subclass are

// always marked "final".

final String title;

@override

_MyHomePageState createState() => _MyHomePageState();

}
```

The state of our **MyHomePage widget** will be defined by the following class. Change it to something like this:

```
class _MyHomePageState extends State<MyHomePage> {

TextStyle style = TextStyle(fontFamily: 'Montserrat', fontSize:
20.0);

@override

Widget build(BuildContext context) {

final emailField = TextField(

obscureText: false,

style: style,

decoration: InputDecoration(

contentPadding: EdgeInsets.fromLTRB(20.0, 15.0, 20.0, 15.0),

hintText: "Email",

border:

OutlineInputBorder(borderRadius: BorderRadius.circular(32.0))),

);

final passwordField = TextField(

obscureText: true,

style: style,

decoration: InputDecoration(

contentPadding: EdgeInsets.fromLTRB(20.0, 15.0, 20.0, 15.0),

hintText: "Password",

border:
```

```
OutlineInputBorder(borderRadius: BorderRadius.circular(32.0))),
);
final loginButon = Material(
elevation: 5.0,
borderRadius: BorderRadius.circular(30.0),
color: Color(0xff01A0C7),
child: MaterialButton(
minWidth: MediaQuery.of(context).size.width,
padding: EdgeInsets.fromLTRB(20.0, 15.0, 20.0, 15.0),
onPressed: () {},
child: Text("Login",
textAlign: TextAlign.center,
style: style.copyWith(
color: Colors.white, fontWeight: FontWeight.bold)),
),
);

return Scaffold(
body: Center(
child: Container(
color: Colors.white,
child: Padding(
padding: const EdgeInsets.all(36.0),
child: Column(
crossAxisAlignment: CrossAxisAlignment.center,
```

```
mainAxisAlignment: MainAxisAlignment.center,
children: <Widget>[
SizedBox(
height: 155.0,
child: Image.asset(
"assets/logo.png",
fit: BoxFit.contain,
),
),
SizedBox(height: 45.0),
emailField,
SizedBox(height: 25.0),
passwordField,
SizedBox(
height: 35.0,
),
loginButon,
SizedBox(
height: 15.0,
),
],
),
),
),
```

```
),
);
}
}
TextStyle style = TextStyle(fontFamily: 'Montserrat', fontSize: 20.0);
```

Now, we create a unique text style that will be applied to our UI elements. As a **fontFamily**, we adopt the Montserrat font. Also, we need to override the construct function that returns our main widget inside the class's body.

Afterwards, we define our user interface elements, which should include two text fields and a login button.

emailField

```
final emailField = TextField(
style: style,
decoration: InputDecoration(
contentPadding: EdgeInsets.fromLTRB(20.0, 15.0, 20.0, 15.0),
hintText: "Email",
border:
OutlineInputBorder(borderRadius: BorderRadius.circular(32.0))),
);
```

The final keyword merely indicates that the object value will not be changed during the app's lifetime. We use the **TextField widget** to create an input, then add a hint, some style, and some decoration. We employ padding to create an empty space within the field's surrounding area. We also include a **borderRadius** to create a rounded input field.

passwordField

```
final passwordField = TextField(
obscureText: true,
style: style,
decoration: InputDecoration(
contentPadding: EdgeInsets.fromLTRB(20.0, 15.0, 20.0, 15.0),
hintText: "Password",
border:
OutlineInputBorder(borderRadius: BorderRadius.circular(32.0))),
);
```

The password field's definition is nearly identical to the previous one, with the exception that we added the property **obscureText: true** to hide input as we type, like a password field should.

loginButton

```
final loginButon = Material(
elevation: 5.0,
borderRadius: BorderRadius.circular(30.0),
color: Color(0xff01A0C7),
child: MaterialButton(
minWidth: MediaQuery.of(context).size.width,
padding: EdgeInsets.fromLTRB(20.0, 15.0, 20.0, 15.0),
onPressed: () {},
child: Text("Login",
textAlign: TextAlign.center,
style: style.copyWith(
color: Colors.white, fontWeight: FontWeight.bold)),
),
);
```

To simply add a **shadow(elevation)** to our button, we use the **Material widget**. To make a rounded button, we additionally add a radius. Finally, we add a button as a child to our **Material widget**, which also accepts a **Text widget**. When our button is clicked, the **onPressed property** is set to **true**, and a function is called.

After that, we combined all of these widgets into our **Scaffold widget**. Within a **Column widget**, our form items are vertically oriented. In most cases, the **SizedBox widget** is just used for spacing purposes. To establish a height for an image, we place it inside a **SizedBox**.

```
return Scaffold(
body: Center(
child: Container(
color: Colors.white,
child: Padding(
padding: const EdgeInsets.all(36.0),
child: Column(
crossAxisAlignment: CrossAxisAlignment.center,
mainAxisAlignment: MainAxisAlignment.center,
children: <Widget>[
SizedBox(
height: 155.0,
child: Image.asset(
"assets/logo.png",
fit: BoxFit.contain,
),
),
SizedBox(height: 45.0),
emailField,
SizedBox(height: 25.0),
passwordField,
```

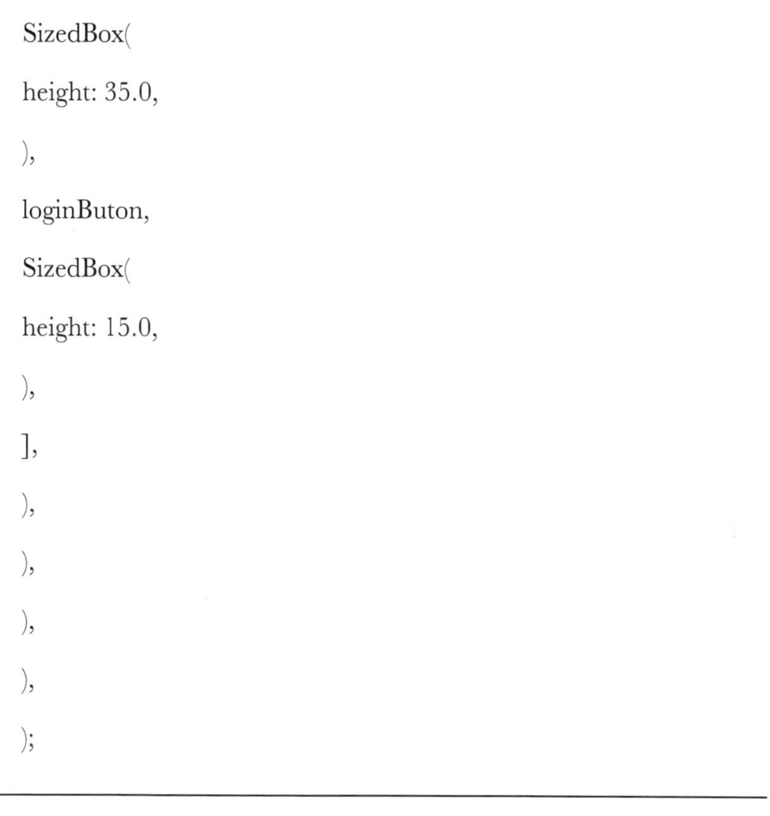

```
SizedBox(
height: 35.0,
),
loginButon,
SizedBox(
height: 15.0,
),
],
),
),
),
),
);
```

The app should be ready to use once everything is completed. If the app isn't currently running, start an Android emulator or an iOS simulator, and run the following command from the project directory's root:

```
flutter run
```

Conclusion

That is all there is to it. You've learned how to make a gorgeous login UI using Flutter in this chapter. You also learned some basic Flutter SDK ideas, and I hope you gained the knowledge you need to continue exploring Flutter. You can find the code used in this tutorial on its GitHub repo at this link:

github.com/Ethiel97/flutter_login_ui

NINE

Flutter Project 4 - Build a Name Generator

We'll write a simple app that generates suggested names for a small business or firm in this chapter. A user should be able to select and unselect names at the end of this project, retaining the right ones. The algorithm generates roughly nine to ten alternatives at a time, and additional names are generated as the user scrolls. A user's ability to scroll is unrestricted.

1. Create a Suitable Flutter Environment

To finish this project, you'll need to have installed the Flutter SDK and an editor. (This is under the presumption that you will be using Android Studio, but if not, please feel free to use whichever editor you want.) You can use any of the following devices to run the codes:

- **A physical Android or iOS device** that has been set to development mode and linked to your computer.
- The **iOS Simulator** (this would require the installation of Xcode tools).
- An **emulator for your Android** (this needs to be setup in Android Studio).

In Chapter 5, we discussed the above-mentioned installation procedures. If you need to refresh your memory, please go check it out once more.

2. Create the Starter Flutter App

Make a simple Flutter app using a template. You can create a project labelled **startup_namer** and migrate to **null safety** as below.

```
$ flutter create startup_namer

$ cd startup_namer

$ dart migrate --apply-changes
```

You'll largely be editing the contents of **lib/main.dart**, which, as you know, contains the Dart code. Substitute all of the code in **lib/main.-dart** with the code below, which shows "Hello World" in the center of your screen.

```
import 'package:flutter/material.dart';

void main() => runApp(MyApp());

class MyApp extends StatelessWidget {

@override

Widget build(BuildContext context) {

return MaterialApp(
```

```
title: 'Welcome to Flutter',
home: Scaffold(
appBar: AppBar(
title: const Text('Welcome to Flutter'),
),
body: const Center(
child: const Text('Hello World'),
),
),
);
}
}
```

Indentation can become twisted when inserting code into your app. The following Flutter tools will help you fix it:

- **IntelliJ DEA/Android Studio:** If you are using this, all you have to do is right-click the Dart code and choose **Reformat Code with dartfmt**.
- **Visual Studio Code:** If you are using this, select **Format Document** from the context menu by right-clicking.
- **Terminal:** Run **flutter format <filename>** to fix any indentation errors.

Now, run the app. Depending on your device, you ought to see Android, iOS, or web output at this point.

3. Use a Third-Party Package

This step will introduce you to the **english_words** open-source package. This includes a few thousand of the most commonly used English terms, as well as several useful functions. The **english_words** package, along with many other open-source packages, can be found at **pub.dev**. A Flutter app's assets are managed using the **pubspec** file. Add **english_words: ^4.0.0** (english_words 4.0.0 or higher) to the dependencies list in **pubspec.yaml**:

```
dependencies:

flutter:

sdk: flutter

cupertino_icons: ^1.0.2

english_words: ^4.0.0 # add this line
```

Click **Packages get** while viewing the pubspec in Android Studio's editing interface. The package is now included in your project. In the console, you should see the following:

```
flutter packages get

Running "flutter packages get" in startup_namer...

Process finished with exit code 0
```

Executing Dart **pub get** also creates a **pubspec.lock file** that contains a list of all packages pulled into the project, along with their version numbers. Import the new package into **lib/main.dart**:

```
import 'package:flutter/material.dart';

import 'package:english_words/english_words.dart'; // Add this line.
```

Android Studio suggests libraries for you to import as you type. It also turns the import string gray, indicating when the imported library isn't being used. Instead of using the usual "Hello World," for this project, utilize the English words package to construct the text and make the following modifications:

```
import 'package:flutter/material.dart';

import 'package:english_words/english_words.dart';

void main() => runApp(MyApp());

class MyApp extends StatelessWidget {

@override

Widget build(BuildContext context) {

final wordPair = WordPair.random(); // Add this line.

return MaterialApp(

title: 'Welcome to Flutter',
```

```
home: Scaffold(
appBar: AppBar(
title: Text('Welcome to Flutter'),
),
body: Center( // Drop the const, and
//child: Text('Hello World'), // Replace this text...
child: Text(wordPair.asPascalCase), // With this text.
),
),
);
}
}
```

If the app is running, hot reload to update the running app. Hot reload works by injecting updated source code files into a Dart Virtual Machine that is already executing (VM). The Flutter framework instantly rebuilds the widget tree once the VM updates classes with new versions of fields and functions, letting you see immediately the effects of your modifications.

The goal of hot reloading is to keep the app running while injecting new versions of the files you edited in the background. You won't lose any state this way, which is especially beneficial if you're experimenting with the UI. To perform a hot reload, type **r** from the command line. You should see a different word pair, picked at random, in the running app each time you click hot reload or save the project. This happens because the word pairing is produced inside the build method whenever the MaterialApp requires rendering or when the platform is toggled in the Flutter Inspector.

Look for typos and correct them if your program isn't working properly.

4. Add a Stateful Widget

In this step, you'll add the **RandomWords stateful widget**, which will produce the **_RandomWordsState State class**. RandomWords will then be used as a child within the existing MyApp stateless widget. Follow the steps below to do so:

Make a Stateful Widget's Boilerplate Code

Outside of MyApp, this can go anywhere in the file, but the solution should put it somewhere at the bottom. Place your cursor after all of the code in **lib/main.dart** and click **Return** a few times to start on a new line. Start typing **stful** in your IDE. At this point, the editor should ask if you want to generate a stateful widget. To accept, press **Return**. The cursor will be set for you to input the name of your stateful widget, and the boilerplate code you would need for two classes should appear.

As the Name of Your Widget, Type RandomWords

The IDE immediately updates the accompanying State class, naming it **_RandomWordsState**, once you've provided RandomWords as the name of the stateful widget. The state class's name is also prefixed with an underscore by default.

The IDE also automatically extends **State<RandomWords>**, showing that you're using a generic State class tailored for RandomWords. The RandomWords widget's state is maintained here, and it contains the majority of the app's functionality. This class saves the created word pair list, which expands infinitely as the user scrolls, and favors word pairs as the user adds or removes them from the list by flicking the heart icon later in this project.

Both classes now have the following appearance:

```
class RandomWords extends StatefulWidget {
@override
_RandomWordsState createState() => _RandomWordsState();
}
class _RandomWordsState extends State<RandomWords> {
@override
Widget build(BuildContext context) {
return Container();
}
}
```

In **_RandomWordsState**, update the **build()** method. Substitute the following two lines for **return Container()**:

```
class _RandomWordsState extends State<RandomWords> {
@override
Widget build(BuildContext context) {
final wordPair = WordPair.random(); // NEW
return Text(wordPair.asPascalCase); // NEW
```

```
}
}
```

Make the following changes to MyApp to remove the word-generation code:

```
class MyApp extends StatelessWidget {
@override
Widget build(BuildContext context) {
final wordPair = WordPair.random(); // DELETE
return MaterialApp(
title: 'Welcome to Flutter',
home: Scaffold(
appBar: AppBar(
title: Text('Welcome to Flutter'),
),
body: Center(
//child: Text(wordPair.asPascalCase), // REPLACE with...
child: RandomWords(), // ...this line
),
),
);
```

```
}
}
```

Hot reload the app once again.

5. Create an Infinite Scrolling ListView

Expand **_RandomWordsState** in this step to generate and display a list of word pairings. The list (displayed in a **ListView widget**) increases indefinitely as the user scrolls. ListView's builder factory constructor allows you to create a list view on demand.

To the **_RandomWordsState** class, add some state variables. Create a **_suggestions** list to keep track of proposed word pairs. Also, add the **_biggerFont** variable to increase the text size.

```
class _RandomWordsState extends State<RandomWords> {
final _suggestions = <WordPair>[]; // NEW
final _biggerFont = const TextStyle(fontSize: 18); // NEW
...
}
```

The **_RandomWordsState** class will then need to have a **_buildSuggestions()** function added to it. This is what creates the **ListView** that displays the word pairing suggestions.

The ListView class has a builder field called **itemBuilder**, which is a factory builder with an anonymous callback function. The function is called with two parameters: the **BuildContext** and the row iterator, **i**. The iterator starts at 0 and increases by 1 for each suggested word combination, each time the function is called. This model allows the user's suggestion list to grow as they scroll down. The complete **_buildSuggestions** function should be added.

Add the following function to the **_RandomWordsState** class, eliminating the comments if you prefer:

```
Widget _buildSuggestions() {
return ListView.builder(
padding: const EdgeInsets.all(16),
// The itemBuilder callback is called once per suggested
// word pairing, and places each suggestion into a ListTile
// row. For even rows, the function adds a ListTile row for
// the word pairing. For odd rows, the function adds a
// Divider widget to visually separate the entries. Note that
// the divider may be difficult to see on smaller devices.
itemBuilder: (BuildContext _context, int i) {
// Add a one-pixel-high divider widget before each row
// in the ListView.
if (i.isOdd) {
return Divider();
}
```

```
// The syntax "i ~/ 2" divides i by 2 and returns an
// integer result.
// For example: 1, 2, 3, 4, 5 becomes 0, 1, 1, 2, 2.
// This calculates the actual number of word pairings
// in the ListView,minus the divider widgets.
final int index = i ~/ 2;
// If you've reached the end of the available word
// pairings...
if (index >= _suggestions.length) {
// ...then generate 10 more and add them to the
// suggestions list.
_suggestions.addAll(generateWordPairs().take(10));
}
return _buildRow(_suggestions[index]);
}
);
}
```

_BuildRow is called once per word pair by the **_buildSuggestions** function. This function creates a **ListTile** for each new pair, allowing you to make the rows more appealing. Also, a **_buildRow** function should be added to **_RandomWordsState**:

```
Widget _buildRow(WordPair pair) {
return ListTile(
title: Text(
pair.asPascalCase,
style: _biggerFont,
),
);
}
```

_RandomWordsState's **construct** method should be updated. Instead of contacting the word-generation library directly, use **_buildSuggestions()**:

```
@override
Widget build(BuildContext context) {
//final wordPair = WordPair.random(); // Delete these...
//return Text(wordPair.asPascalCase); // ... two lines.

return Scaffold ( // Add from here...
appBar: AppBar(
title: Text('Startup Name Generator'),
),
body: _buildSuggestions(),
```

```
); // ... to here.
}
```

Change the title of **MyApp**, remove the **AppBar**, and change the home property to a **RandomWords widget** in the **build function**.

```
@override
Widget build(BuildContext context) {
return MaterialApp(
title: 'Startup Name Generator',
home: RandomWords(),
);
}
```

Run the application. Regardless of how far you scroll, you should see a list of word combinations.

6. Add Icons to the List

You'll add heart icons to each row in this phase. You'll make them tappable, and save the favorites in the next stage. To **_RandomWords-State**, add a **_saved Set**. The user's liked word pairs are saved in this Set. Since a correctly constructed Set does not allow duplicate entries, it is preferable over a List.

```
class _RandomWordsState extends State<RandomWords> {

final _suggestions = <WordPair>[];

final _saved = <WordPair>{}; // NEW

final _biggerFont = TextStyle(fontSize: 18.0);

...

}
```

Add an **alreadySaved** check to the **_buildRow** function to ensure that a word pairing hasn't already been saved to favorites.

```
Widget _buildRow(WordPair pair) {

final alreadySaved = _saved.contains(pair); // NEW

...

}
```

You'll also add heart-shaped icons to the **ListTile** objects in **_buildRow()** to enable liking. The ability to interact with the heart icons will be included in the next step.

After the text, add the icons as seen below:

```
Widget _buildRow(WordPair pair) {
final alreadySaved = _saved.contains(pair);
return ListTile(
title: Text(
pair.asPascalCase,
style: _biggerFont,
),
trailing: Icon( // NEW from here...
alreadySaved ? Icons.favorite : Icons.favorite_border,
color: alreadySaved ? Colors.red : null,
), // ... to here.
);
}
```

Hot reload the app. Each row should now have open hearts.

7. Activating Interactivity

The heart icons will be made tappable in this step. When a user taps an entry in the list to toggle between likes, that word combination is added to or removed from a saved favorites list.

To make this possible, you'll need to change the **_buildRow** method. If you've already added a word entry to your favorites, touching it again removes it. The function executes **setState()** when a tile is pressed to alert the framework that the status has changed.

As illustrated below, add **onTap** to the **_buildRow** method:

```
Widget _buildRow(WordPair pair) {
final alreadySaved = _saved.contains(pair);
return ListTile(
title: Text(
pair.asPascalCase,
style: _biggerFont,
),
trailing: Icon(
alreadySaved ? Icons.favorite : Icons.favorite_border,
color: alreadySaved ? Colors.red : null,
),
onTap: () { // NEW lines from here...
setState(() {
if (alreadySaved) {
_saved.remove(pair);
} else {
_saved.add(pair);
}
```

```
});
}, // ... to here.
);
}
```

Hot reload the app. You should be able to favorite or unfavorite an entry by tapping any tile. Now when you tap a tile, an ink splash motion should appear from the tap spot.

8. Navigating to a New Screen

The Navigator in Flutter is in charge of a stack that contains the app's routes. The presentation of a route is updated when it is pushed into the Navigator's stack. When you select a route from the Navigator's stack, the display returns to the previous route.

In the build function for **_RandomWordsState**, you'll then add a list icon to the AppBar. When the user hits the list icon, a new route is delivered to the Navigator, containing the saved favorites and showing the icon. To the build method, add the icon and its accompanying action:

```
class _RandomWordsState extends State<RandomWords> {
...
@override
Widget build(BuildContext context) {
return Scaffold(
appBar: AppBar(
```

```
title: Text('Startup Name Generator'),
actions: [
IconButton(icon: Icon(Icons.list), onPressed: _pushSaved),
],
),
body: _buildSuggestions(),
);
}
...
}
```

As illustrated by the square brackets, certain widget attributes take *a single* widget (child), whereas others, such as action, take *an array* of widgets (children) **([])**. The **_RandomWordsState** class now includes a **_pushSaved()** function.

```
void _pushSaved() {
}
```

Hot reload the app. In the app bar, the list icon is displayed. Since the **_pushSaved** function is now empty, tapping this at this point has no effect. You'll need to create a route and add it to the Navigator's stack. The screen should change to show the new path as a result of this activity. In an anonymous function, the content for the new page is built in **MaterialPageRoute**'s builder property.

As demonstrated here, **Navigator.push** pushes the route to the Navigator's stack. The IDE will warn you that your code is invalid, but you'll solve that in the next section.

```
void _pushSaved() {
Navigator.of(context).push(
);
}
```

The **MaterialPageRoute** and associated constructor will now be added. Include the code for creating the **ListTile** rows. ListTile's **divideTiles()** function creates a horizontal gap between ListTiles. The final rows are stored in the split variable, which was transformed to a list via the toList convenience function **()**. As demonstrated below, add the following code:

```
void _pushSaved() {
Navigator.of(context).push(
MaterialPageRoute<void>(
// NEW lines from here...
builder: (BuildContext context) {
final tiles = _saved.map(
```

```
(WordPair pair) {
return ListTile(
title: Text(
pair.asPascalCase,
style: _biggerFont,
),
);
},
);
final divided = tiles.isNotEmpty
? ListTile.divideTiles(context: context, tiles: tiles).toList()
: <Widget>[];
return Scaffold(
appBar: AppBar(
title: Text('Saved Suggestions'),
),
body: ListView(children: divided),
);
}, // ...to here.
),
);
}
```

The new route named **SavedSuggestions** is returned by the builder property when it returns the Scaffold containing that app bar. The new route's body is made up of a ListView that contains the ListTiles rows. A separator runs down the middle of each row.

Reload the app quickly. Choose some of your favorites, and press the list button in the app bar to add them to your favorites list. The favorites are included in the new route. The Navigator modifies the app bar by adding a **Back** button. Tap the back button to return to the home route.

9. Modify the UI With Themes

You'll change the theme of the app at this phase. The theme determines how your app looks and feels. You can alter the theme to fit your branding or utilize the default theme, which is dependent on the physical device or emulator you're using.

By specifying the **ThemeData** class, you may simply modify an app's theme. The app will use the default theme, but the primary color should be changed to white from the **MyApp** class:

```
class MyApp extends StatelessWidget {
@override
Widget build(BuildContext context) {
return MaterialApp(
title: 'Startup Name Generator',
theme: ThemeData( // Add the 3 lines from here...
primaryColor: Colors.white,
), // ... to here.
home: RandomWords(),
```

```
);
}
}
```

Conclusion

Hot reload the app one last time. The entire background of the finished app, including the app bar, should be white. The colors class in the Material library provides many color constants that you can play with.

We just completed another Flutter app that runs on iOS and Android by writing Dart code, using hot reload for a faster development cycle, and implementing a stateful widget to add interactivity to the app. We also created a route, added logic for moving between the home route and the new route, and changed the look of the app's UI using themes. Hopefully, you learned a thing or two. We'll look at one more project using flutter in the next chapter.

TEN

Flutter Project 5 - Build an Ecommerce App

This chapter will focus on using Flutter to create an ecommerce app. Simply put, **ecommerce** (electronic commerce) is the buying and selling of goods and services, as well as the transmission of payments or data, over an electronic network, most commonly the internet. Business-to-business (B2B), business-to-consumer (B2C), consumer-to-consumer, and consumer-to-business transactions are all possible. Since the Flutter language allows for the construction of ecommerce mobile apps, we'll explore the creation of one in this chapter.

1. Set Up Your Environment

This step presupposes that you have already installed the Flutter SDK. Also, we'll be using the Visual Studio Code editor for this, and as such, its plugins should be set up in your environment. If you need any help doing this, revert to the fifth chapter of this book.

2. Create Your Flutter Project

Now to begin, we must create a project with the name **fluttercommerce** in Visual Studio Code. Follow these procedures to create this new project in Visual Studio Code:

- Select **View → Command Palette** from the menu bar.
- Select **Flutter: New Project** after typing "flutter."
- Press Enter after entering a project name, such as "**fluttercommerce**."
- Create or choose the parent directory for the new project folder.
- Allow for the completion of the project creation process and the appearance of the **main.dart** file.

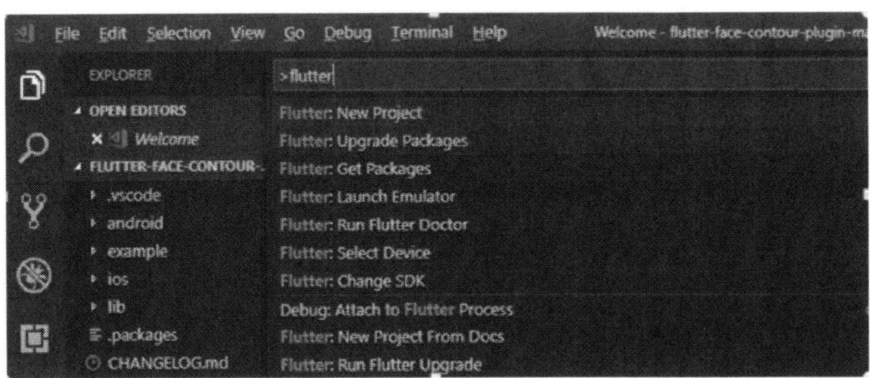

3. Import Your Package

Add the **intl** and **uuid** packages to your project after that. This is what your **pubspec.yaml** file should look like:

```
name: flutterecommerse

description: A new Flutter project.

# The following defines the version and build number for your application.
```

```
# A version number is three numbers separated by dots, like 1.2.43

# followed by an optional build number separated by a +.

# Both the version and the builder number may be overridden in flutter

# build by specifying --build-name and --build-number, respectively.

# In Android, build-name is used as versionName while build-number used as versionCode.

# Read more about Android versioning at https://developer.android.com/studio/publish/versioning

# In iOS, build-name is used as CFBundleShortVersionString while build-number used as CFBundleVersion.

# Read more about iOS versioning at

# https://developer.apple.com/library/archive/documentation/General/Reference/InfoPlistKeyReference/Articles/CoreFoundationKeys.html

version: 1.0.0+1

environment:

sdk: ">=2.1.0 <3.0.0"

dependencies:

flutter:

sdk: flutter

# The following adds the Cupertino Icons font to your application.

# Use with the CupertinoIcons class for iOS style icons.
```

cupertino_icons: ^0.1.2

intl: ^0.15.8

uuid: 2.0.0

dev_dependencies:

flutter_test:

sdk: flutter

For information on the generic Dart part of this file, see the

following page: https://dart.dev/tools/pub/pubspec

The following section is specific to Flutter.

flutter:

The following line ensures that the Material Icons font is

included with your application, so that you can use the icons in

the material Icons class.

uses-material-design: true

To add assets to your application, add an assets section, like this:

assets:

- images/a_dot_burr.jpeg

- images/a_dot_ham.jpeg

An image asset can refer to one or more resolution-specific "variants", see

https://flutter.dev/assets-and-images/#resolution-aware.

For details regarding adding assets from package dependencies, see

```
# https://flutter.dev/assets-and-images/#from-packages

# To add custom fonts to your application, add a fonts section here,

# in this "flutter" section. Each entry in this list should have a

# "family" key with the font family name, and a "fonts" key with a

# list giving the asset and other descriptors for the font. For

# example:

# fonts:

# - family: Schyler

# fonts:

# - asset: fonts/Schyler-Regular.ttf

# - asset: fonts/Schyler-Italic.ttf

# style: italic

# - family: Trajan Pro

# fonts:

# - asset: fonts/TrajanPro.ttf

# - asset: fonts/TrajanPro_Bold.ttf

# weight: 700

# For details regarding fonts from package dependencies,

# see https://flutter.dev/custom-fonts/#from-packages
```

Then, in the command palette, we select "**get package**" and wait for the procedure to complete. We need to develop data modeling after we create **pubspec.yaml**. So make a new directory for models files in **[projectname]/lib/[modelname]**. We'll then create **item.dart** with the following static data:

```
import 'package:flutter/material.dart';

import 'package:intl/intl.dart';

class Item {

String id;

String name;

String description;

int price;

bool inStock;

String imageUrl;

Item(

{this.id,

this.name,

this.description,

this.price,

this.inStock,

this.imageUrl});

String get formattedAvailability => inStock ? "Available" : "Out of stock";

String get formattedPrice => Item.formatter.format(this.price);

Color get availabilityColor => inStock ? Colors.grey : Colors.red;

static final formatter =

NumberFormat.currency(locale: 'id_ID', symbol: "Rp ");
```

```
static List<Item> get dummyItems => [

Item(

id: "1",

name: "iPhone X (Product RED) ",

description: 'More magical than ever.',

price: 12499999,

inStock: true,

imageUrl:

'https://store.storeimages.cdn-apple.com/4982/as-
images.apple.com/is/image/AppleInc/aos/published/images/i/
ph/iphone/xr/iphone-xr-red-select-201809?
wid=940&hei=1112&fmt=png-
alpha&qlt=80&.v=1551226038669'),

Item(

id: "2",

name: "AirPods with Wireless Charging Case",

description: 'More magical than ever.',

price: 2999999,

inStock: true,

imageUrl:

'https://store.storeimages.cdn-apple.com/4982/as-
images.apple.com/is/image/AppleInc/aos/published/images/
M/RX/MRXJ2/MRXJ2?
wid=1144&hei=1144&fmt=jpeg&qlt=95&op_usm=0.5%2C0.5&
.v=1551489675083'),

Item(
```

```
id: "3",

name: "iPhone X Max (GOLD)",

description: 'More magical than ever.',

price: 18999999,

inStock: true,

imageUrl:

'https://store.storeimages.cdn-apple.com/4982/as-
images.apple.com/is/image/AppleInc/aos/published/images/i/
ph/iphone/xs/iphone-xs-max-gold-select-2018?
wid=940&hei=1112&fmt=png-
alpha&qlt=80&.v=1550795409154'),

Item(

id: "4",

name: "iPhone X (SILVER)",

description: 'More magical than ever.',

price: 14999999,

inStock: true,

imageUrl:

'https://store.storeimages.cdn-apple.com/4982/as-
images.apple.com/is/image/AppleInc/aos/published/images/i/
ph/iphone/xs/iphone-xs-silver-select-2018?
wid=940&hei=1112&fmt=png-
alpha&qlt=80&.v=1550795411708'),

Item(

id: "5",

name: "iPad Pro (SPACE GRAY)",
```

```
description: 'More magical than ever.',

price: 13999999,

inStock: true,

imageUrl:

'https://store.storeimages.cdn-apple.com/4982/as-images.apple.com/is/image/AppleInc/aos/published/images/i/pa/ipad/pro/ipad-pro-11-select-cell-spacegray-201810?wid=940&hei=1112&fmt=png-alpha&qlt=80&.v=1540591731427'),

Item(

id: "6",

name: "Apple Watch Silver Aluminum (44 mm)",

description: 'More magical than ever.',

price: 8999999,

inStock: false,

imageUrl:

'https://store.storeimages.cdn-apple.com/4982/as-images.apple.com/is/image/AppleInc/aos/published/images/4/4/44/alu/44-alu-silver-sport-white-s4-1up?wid=940&hei=1112&fmt=png-alpha&qlt=80&.v=1539190366920'),

];

}
```

Create **shopping_cart.dart** afterwards, as things will need to be purchased:

```
import 'item.dart';
import 'package:uuid/uuid.dart';
class ShoppingCart {
final orderId = Uuid().v4();
List<Item> items = [];
bool get isEmpty => items.isEmpty;
int get numOfItems => items.length;
int get totalPrice {
int totalPrice = 0;
items.forEach((i) {
totalPrice += i.price;
});
return totalPrice;
}
String get formattedTotalPrice {
if (isEmpty) {
return Item.formatter.format(0);
}
return Item.formatter.format(this.totalPrice);
}
bool isExists(item) {
if (items.isEmpty) {
```

```
return false;
}
final indexOfItem = items.indexWhere((i) => item.id == i.id);
return indexOfItem >= 0;
}
void add(Item item) {
if (items.isEmpty) {
items.add(item);
return;
}
if (!this.isExists(item)) {
items.add(item);
}
}
void remove(Item item) {
if (items.isEmpty) return;
final indexOfItem = items.indexWhere((i) => item.id == i.id);
if (indexOfItem >= 0) {
items.removeAt(indexOfItem);
}
}
Map<String, dynamic> get toMap {
final List<Map<String, dynamic>> items = this
```

```
.items
.map((i) => {
'id': i.id,
'name': i.name,
'description': i.description,
'price': i.price,
'inStock': i.inStock,
'imageUrl': i.imageUrl
})
.toList();
return {"orderId": this.orderId, "items": items, "total": this.totalPrice};
}
}
```

Then, if we're going to cart some products till checkout, we'll need the **services** class to process them. As a result, we construct display class items like the ones below:

```
import 'package:flutter/material.dart';
import 'cart_list.dart';
import 'models/shopping_cart.dart';
```

```
import 'models/item.dart';

class ShopListWidget extends StatefulWidget {

@override

State<StatefulWidget> createState() {

return _ShopListState();

}

}

class _ShopListState extends State<ShopListWidget> {

ShoppingCart cart = ShoppingCart();

final _scaffoldKey = GlobalKey<ScaffoldState>();

final List<Item> items = Item.dummyItems;

@override

Widget build(BuildContext context) {

final columnCount =

MediaQuery.of(context).orientation == Orientation.portrait ?
2 : 4;

final width = MediaQuery.of(context).size.width / columnCount;

const height = 400;

List<Widget> items = [];

for (var x = 0; x < this.items.length; x++) {

bool isSideLine;

if (columnCount == 2) {

isSideLine = x % 2 == 0;

} else {
```

```
isSideLine = x % 4 != 3;
}
final item = this.items[x];
items.add(_ShopListItem(
item: item,
isInCart: cart.isExists(item),
isSideLine: isSideLine,
onTap: (item) {
_scaffoldKey.currentState.hideCurrentSnackBar();
if (cart.isExists(item)) {
cart.remove(item);
_scaffoldKey.currentState.showSnackBar(SnackBar(
content: Text('Item is removed from cart!'),
));
} else if (item.inStock) {
cart.add(item);
_scaffoldKey.currentState.showSnackBar(SnackBar(
content: Text('Item is added to cart!'),
));
} else {
_scaffoldKey.currentState.showSnackBar(SnackBar(
content: Text('Item is out of stock!'),
));
```

```
}
this.setState(() {});
},
));
}
return Scaffold(
key: _scaffoldKey,
appBar: AppBar(
title: Text("Apple Store"),
),
body: GridView.count(
childAspectRatio: width / height,
scrollDirection: Axis.vertical,
crossAxisCount: columnCount,
children: items,
),
floatingActionButton: cart.isEmpty
? null
: FloatingActionButton.extended(
onPressed: () {
Navigator.of(context).push(MaterialPageRoute(
builder: (context) => CartListWidget(
cart: this.cart,
```

```
)));
},
icon: Icon(Icons.shopping_cart),
label: Text("${cart.numOfItems}"),
));
}
}
class _ShopListItem extends StatelessWidget {
final Item item;
final bool isInCart;
final bool isSideLine;
dynamic onTap;
_ShopListItem({this.item, this.isInCart, this.isSideLine, this.onTap});
@override
Widget build(BuildContext context) {
Border border;
if (isSideLine) {
border = Border(
bottom: BorderSide(color: Colors.grey, width: 0.5),
right: BorderSide(color: Colors.grey, width: 0.5));
} else {
border = Border(bottom: BorderSide(color: Colors.grey, width: 0.5));
```

```
}
return InkWell(
onTap: () => this.onTap(item),
child: Container(
decoration: BoxDecoration(border: border),
child: Column(
crossAxisAlignment: CrossAxisAlignment.center,
children: <Widget>[
Padding(
padding: EdgeInsets.only(top: 16),
),
Container(
child: AspectRatio(
aspectRatio: 1,
child: Image.network(item.imageUrl),
),
height: 250,
),
Padding(
padding: EdgeInsets.only(top: 16),
),
Text(item.name,
textAlign: TextAlign.center,
```

```
style: Theme.of(context)
.textTheme
.title
.apply(fontSizeFactor: 0.8)),
Padding(
padding: EdgeInsets.only(top: 16),
),
Text(item.formattedPrice,
textAlign: TextAlign.center,
style: Theme.of(context)
.textTheme
.subhead
.apply(fontSizeFactor: 0.8)),
Padding(
padding: EdgeInsets.only(top: 16),
),
Text(this.isInCart ? "In Cart" : item.formattedAvailability,
textAlign: TextAlign.center,
style: Theme.of(context).textTheme.caption.apply(
fontSizeFactor: 0.8,
color:
isInCart ? Colors.blue : item.availabilityColor)),
],
```

```
)));
}
}
```

Create **cart_list.dart** to display items for checkout:

```
import 'dart:async';
import 'package:flutter/material.dart';
import 'package:flutter/services.dart';
import 'models/shopping_cart.dart';
import 'models/item.dart';
class CartListWidget extends StatefulWidget {
final ShoppingCart cart;
CartListWidget({this.cart});
@override
State<StatefulWidget> createState() {
return _CartListWidgetState();
}
}
class _CartListWidgetState extends State<CartListWidget> {
static const platform = const
MethodChannel('camellabs.com/payment');
```

```
Future<void> _checkout() async {
await platform.invokeMethod('charge', widget.cart.toMap);
}
@override
Widget build(BuildContext context) {
List<Widget> items = [];
widget.cart.items.forEach((c) {
items.add(_CartListItemWidget(
item: c,
));
items.add(Padding(
padding: EdgeInsets.only(top: 8.0),
));
});
return Scaffold(
appBar: AppBar(
title: Text('My Cart'),
actions: <Widget>[
FlatButton(
textColor: Colors.white,
onPressed: () => this._checkout(),
child: Text("Checkout"),
)
```

```
],
),
body: Container(
decoration: BoxDecoration(color: Color(0xfff0eff4)),
child: Stack(
children: <Widget>[
ListView(
padding: EdgeInsets.only(bottom: 64),
children: items,
),
Positioned(
bottom: 0,
left: 0,
right: 0,
height: 64,
child: _CartListSummaryFooterWidget(
totalPrice: widget.cart.formattedTotalPrice,
),
)
],
)));
}
}
```

```
class _CartListSummaryFooterWidget extends StatelessWidget {
final String totalPrice;
_CartListSummaryFooterWidget({this.totalPrice});
@override
Widget build(BuildContext context) {
return Container(
decoration: BoxDecoration(
color: Color(0XFFF4F4F4),
border: Border(top: BorderSide(color: Colors.grey, width: 0.5))),
child: Padding(
padding: EdgeInsets.all(16.0),
child: Center(
child: Row(
children: <Widget>[
Text(
'Total',
textAlign: TextAlign.left,
style: Theme.of(context).textTheme.title,
),
Expanded(
child: Text(
this.totalPrice,
textAlign: TextAlign.right,
```

```
style: Theme.of(context).textTheme.subhead,
))
],
)),
));
}
}
class _CartListItemWidget extends StatelessWidget {
final Item item;
_CartListItemWidget({this.item});
@override
Widget build(BuildContext context) {
return Container(
decoration: BoxDecoration(
color: Colors.white,
border: Border(
top: BorderSide(color: Colors.grey, width: 0.5),
bottom: BorderSide(color: Colors.grey, width: 0.5))),
padding: EdgeInsets.all(16.0),
child: Row(
children: <Widget>[
Container(
height: 64,
child: AspectRatio(
```

```
aspectRatio: 1,
child: Image.network(item.imageUrl),
),
),
Padding(
padding: EdgeInsets.only(right: 8.0),
),
Expanded(
child: Text(
item.name,
style:
Theme.of(context).textTheme.title.apply(fontSizeFactor: 0.75),
)),
Padding(
padding: EdgeInsets.only(right: 8.0),
),
Text(
item.formattedPrice,
textAlign: TextAlign.right,
style: Theme.of(context).textTheme.subhead,
)
],
),
);
```

```
}
}
```

4. Create Your Main.dart

The final step is to generate **main.dart**, which should look like this:

```
import 'package:flutter/material.dart';
import 'shop_list.dart';
void main() => runApp(MyApp());
class MyApp extends StatelessWidget {
@override
Widget build(BuildContext context) {
return MaterialApp(
title: 'ShopX',
debugShowCheckedModeBanner: false,
theme: ThemeData(
primarySwatch: Colors.blue,
),
home: ShopListWidget(),
);
}
}
```

At this point, the application can be run to display the appropriate output, as shown below:

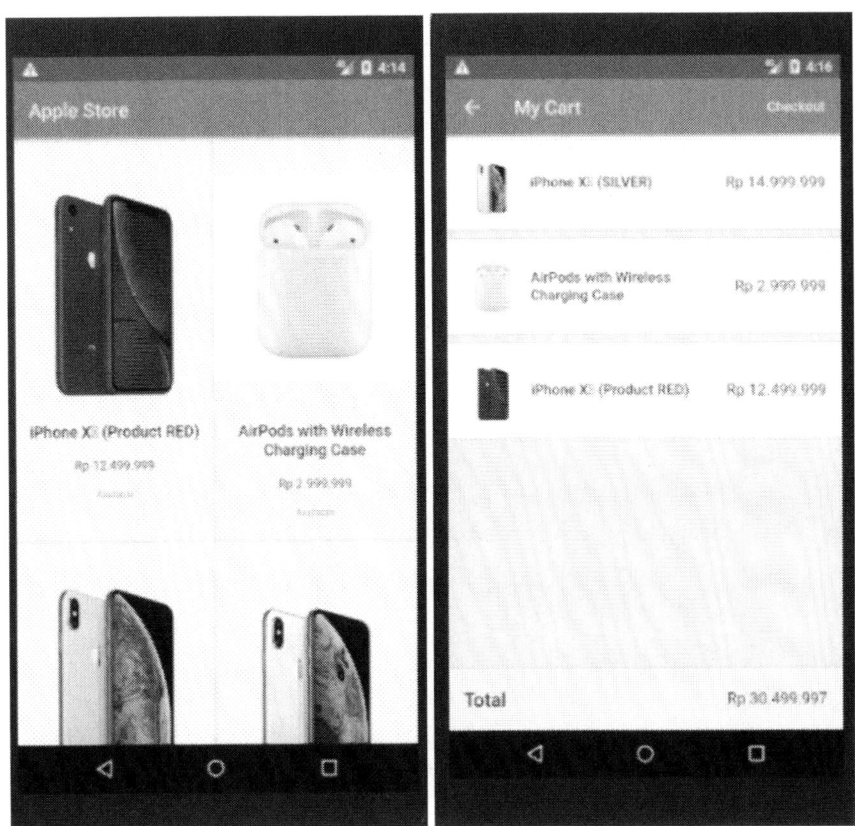

Conclusion

I hope you have found this project useful. For the complete source code used here, check out the flutter ecommerce GitHub:

github.com/eccosuprastyo/flutter/tree/master/flutterecommerse

ELEVEN

FlutterFlow Project 1 - Build a Threefold Pricing Scroll

FlutterFlow is an online low-code builder for native mobile apps. It has a simple drag-and-drop interface that lets you build a fully functional app in as little as an hour. You can have stateful elements and add actions to various parts of your app to create/update/delete records. You can also load data dynamically.

Developers can quickly handle user authentication, create data types in the software's editor, and link widgets to the Firebase database, thanks to Google's Firebase integration. Its a low- to no-code development platform software boasting features like:

- Access Control
- Mobile Development
- Testing Management
- Workflow Management
- Drag and drop Builder
- App Integrations
- Integrations Management
- Application Templates
- Code Assistance
- Debugging

- Version Control
- Web Development
- Machine Learning
- AI-Assisted Development
- Extension Programming

In this chapter, we will build a threefold pricing page scroll using FlutterFlow.

1. Set Up Your Environment

FlutterFlow integrates with Firebase, both for user authentication and connecting the UI to a database. Firebase is accessed through a number of different libraries, one for each Firebase product (e.g. Realtime Database, Authentication, Analytics, or Cloud Storage). Please refer to the official FlutterFlow instructions here www.youtube.com/watch?v=vVTIafL7tw0 to set up the integration with Firebase.

2. Create a New Page

The first thing we're going to do is create a new page on boarding two, give it a name and a link.

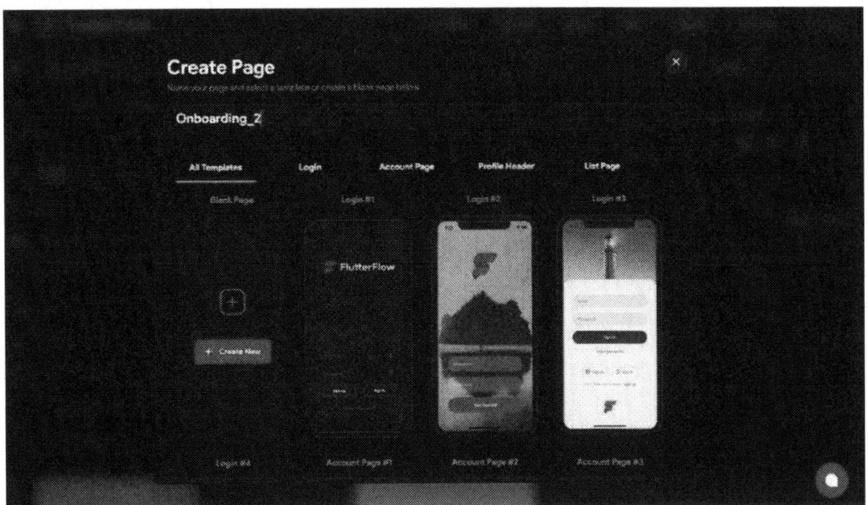

The newly created page should look like this:

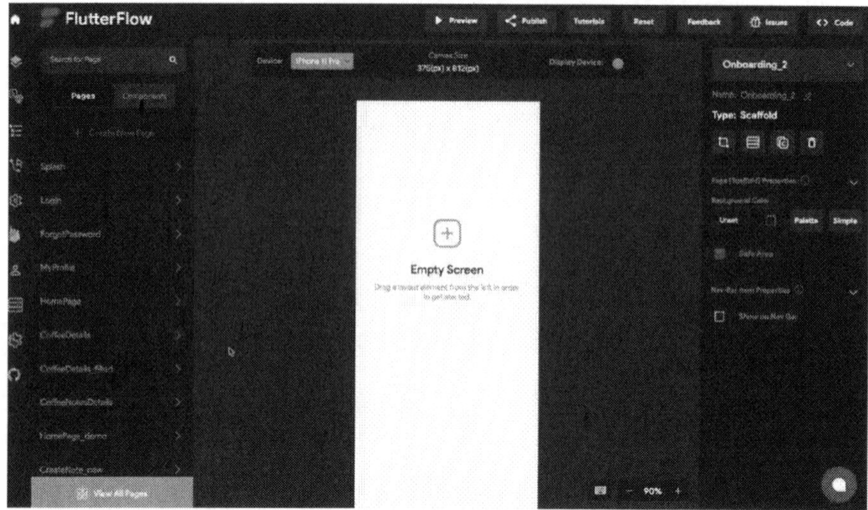

3. Begin To Reposition Your Widgets To Build

To design a full featured mobile app with FlutterFlow, you can use a variety of tools. Images, buttons, icons, and lists can be used by app developers to make the final product more appealing and clear. There are a variety of layouts to pick from depending on the user's requirements.

Now what we're going to do here is drag over the column. What I'm doing is using **command+F** to find a widget in the left Sidebar and then dragging it over to the middle. First we do the column, then the row, and then the page view.

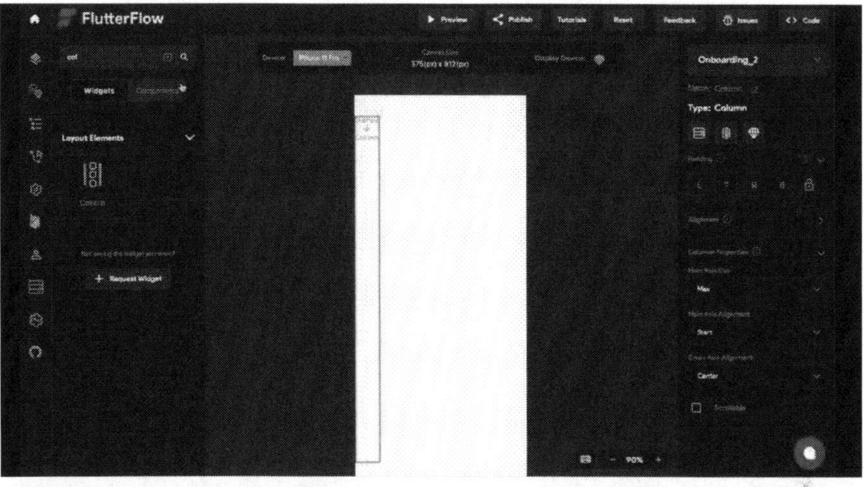

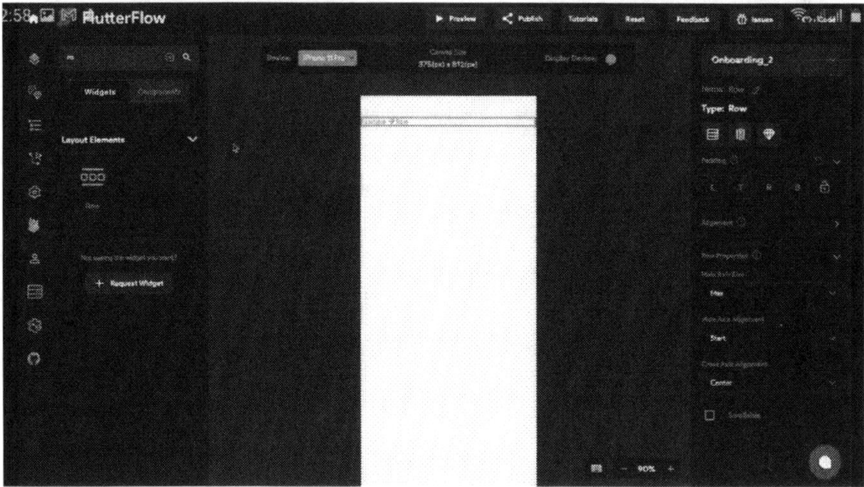

Put that page view in the row. We're going to edit this out a little bit. W"re going to get rid of the safe area of the page. That way, we can span the entirety of the page. We're going to change the Scroll action for the page view to vertical.

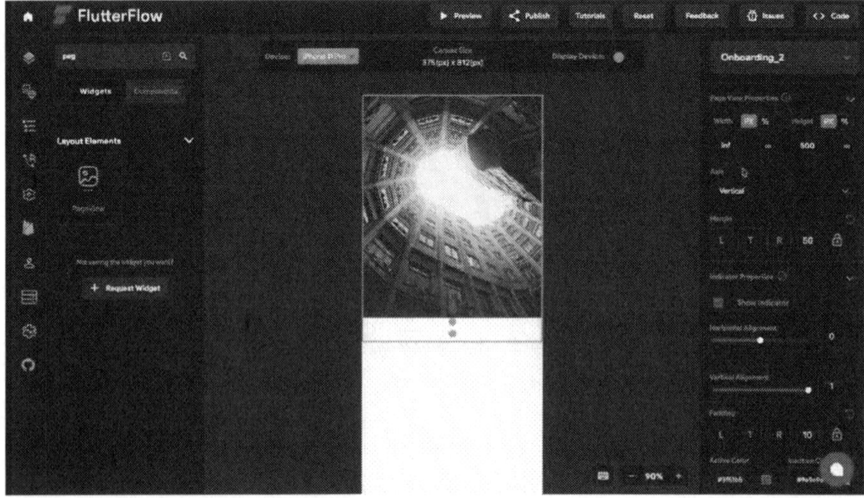

And then we're gonna just mix up the indicator position to the top left with the alignment sliders. You can also just enter the values here—you don't have to use the sliders.

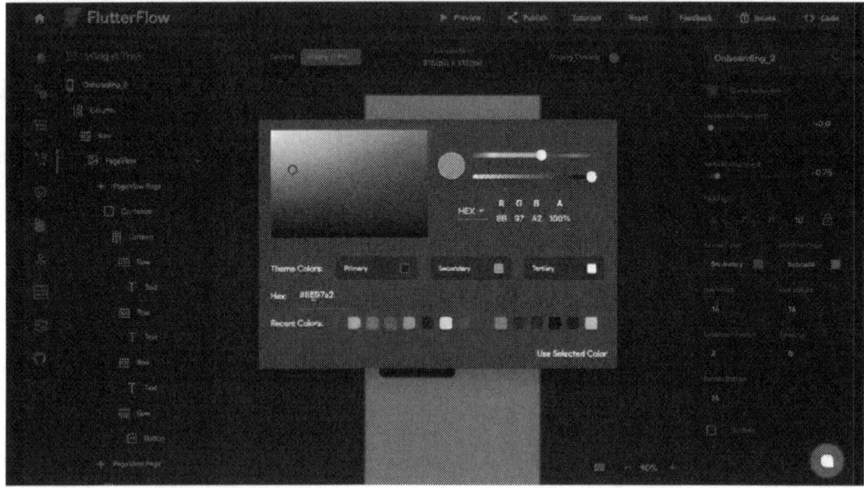

Then we're going to edit the design of the indicators themselves. Next, we'll select the page view and set the height to a percentage—just make it 100% as seen below:

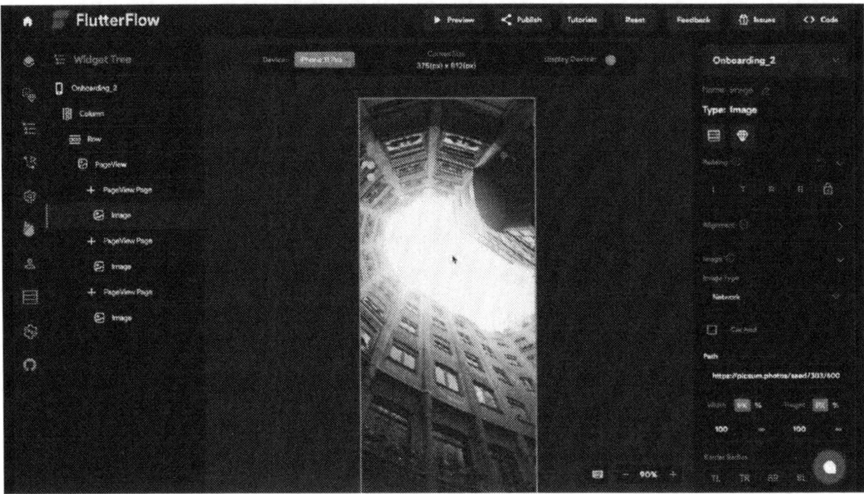

After this, we can get rid of this image, replacing it with what we want in this page view. So we're going to drag a container on there, and then again a column and a row.

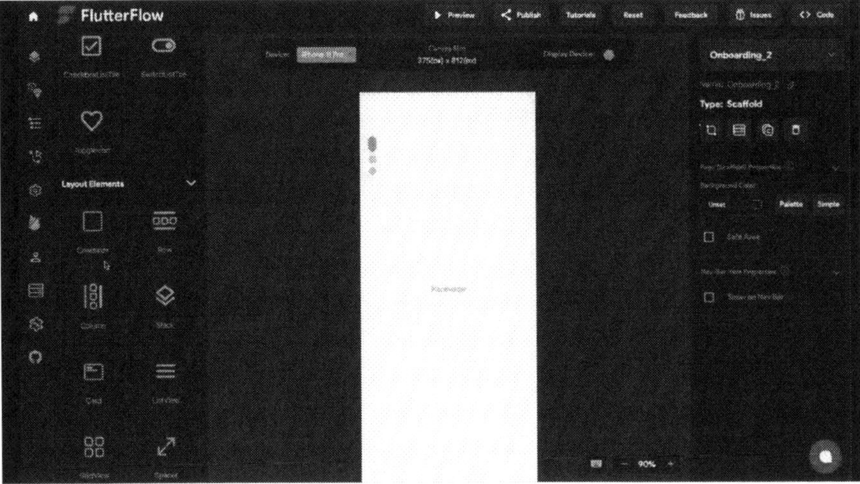

This will just align our content in the middle of the column, rather than at the beginning or the start. So let's go ahead and grab the background color we need for this.

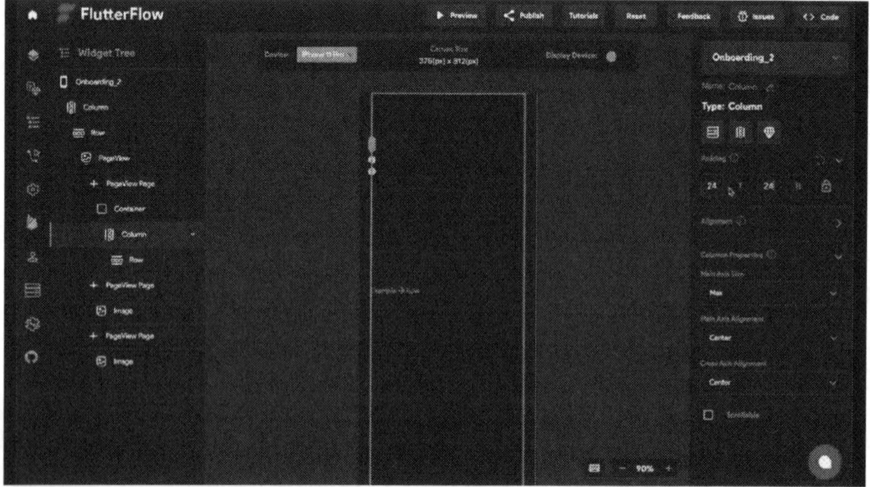

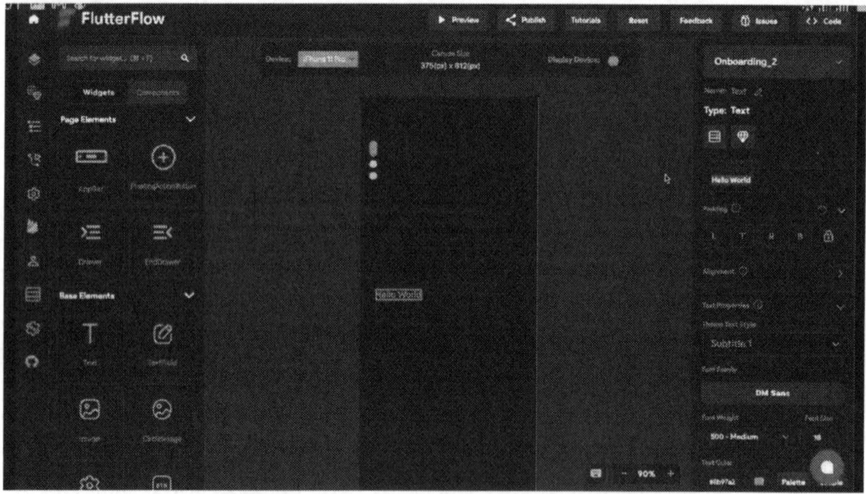

Make sure the container is selected. Enter that value there. And then just press enter.

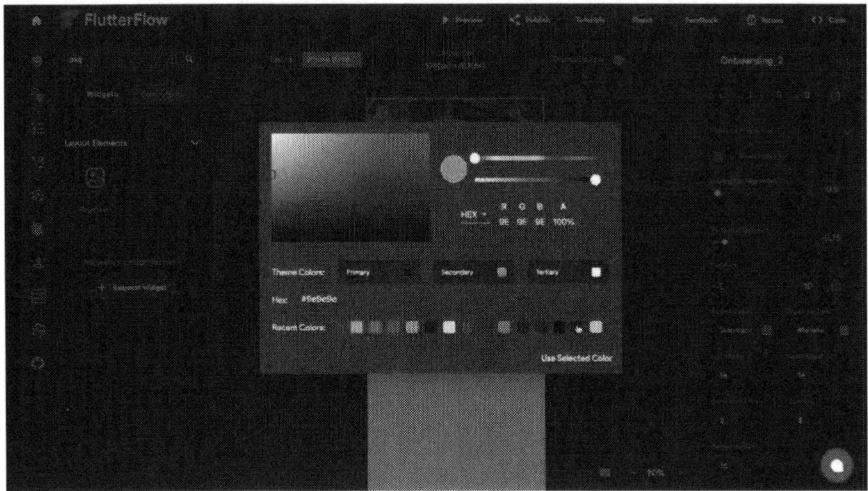

Note: in FlutterFlow, when you enter a custom value, you may need to press enter for it to capture that value. (This is a known bug at the time of writing.)

Now, we double check to make sure our spacing is accurate. We'll also add some text here.

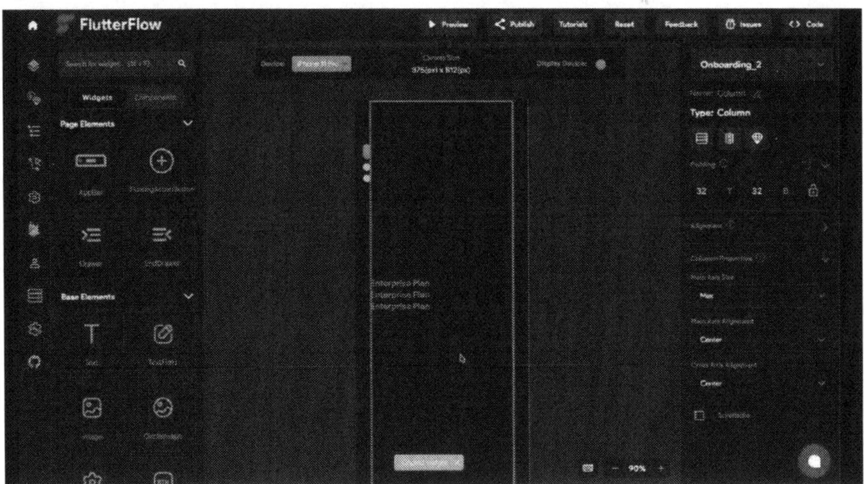

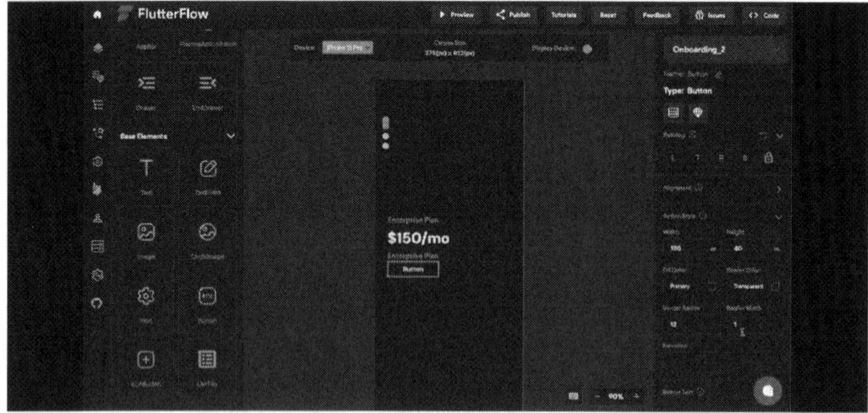

After this, we'll go ahead and copy that row. It's very easy. Just select the row itself, and then make sure that you're in the parent of that row—which in this case is the column. And then you can paste it in there.

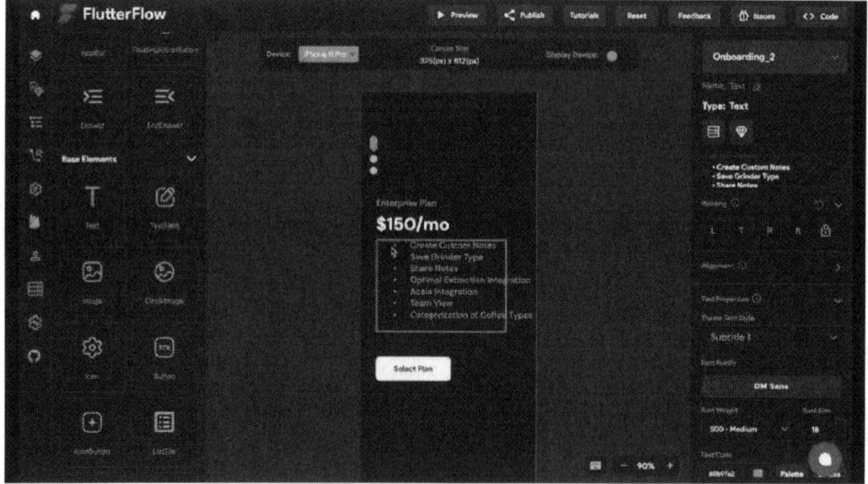

You can't paste a *row* within a *row*, but you can paste a *child* within a *parent*, which is highly beneficial. We're going to add a button over here and give it a custom design. We'll also set the stylization of this button to match our design. If necessary, go ahead and give the design a little more padding vertically.

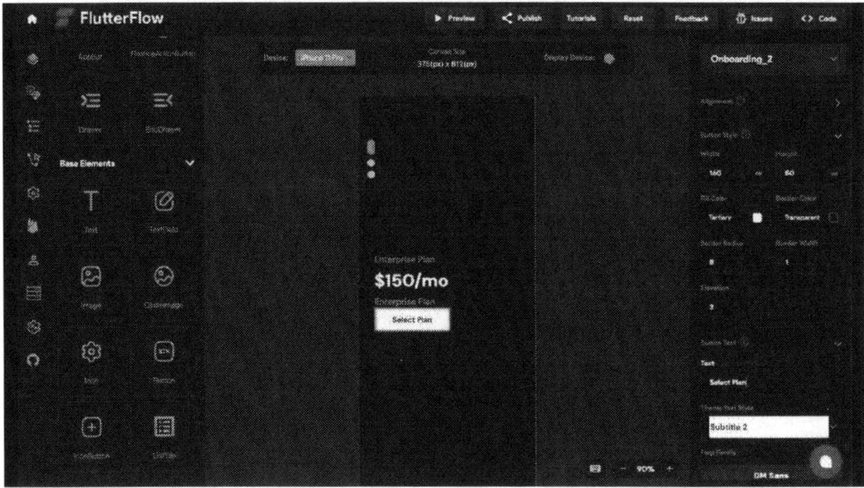

Right. Now, we'll copy the text we want to reflect on our final page. Paste this text right below the subscription amount and month:

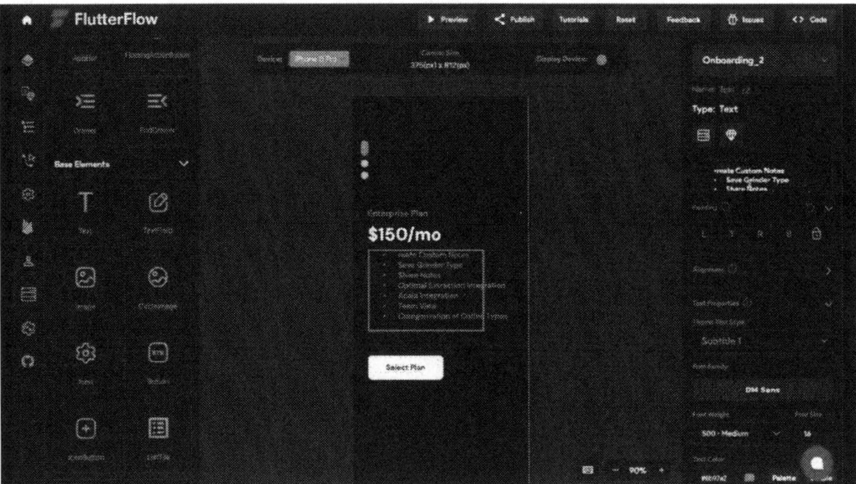

We're going to decrease the size of the text font to make it all look a little better.

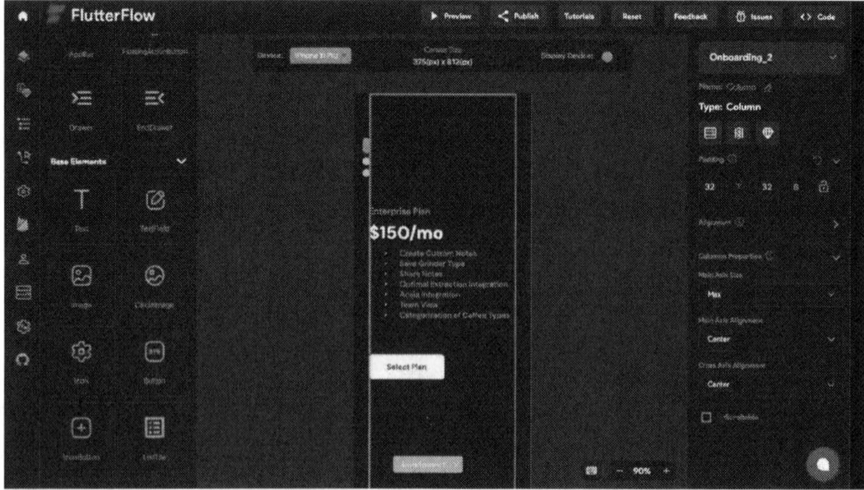

Again, add some padding to the top to lengthen and balance out. Now that this page is done, we'll copy the column itself, so that we can get to a new page view and begin work on the second page.

Paste the column in there, then your text in the centre.

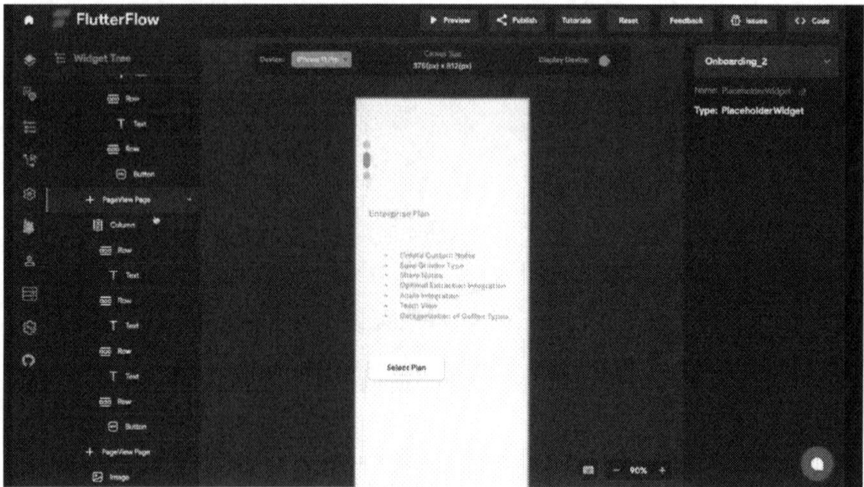

Let's set the background color to white. We'll change the color of our header and use black button design. Make sure your indicator is the proper color.

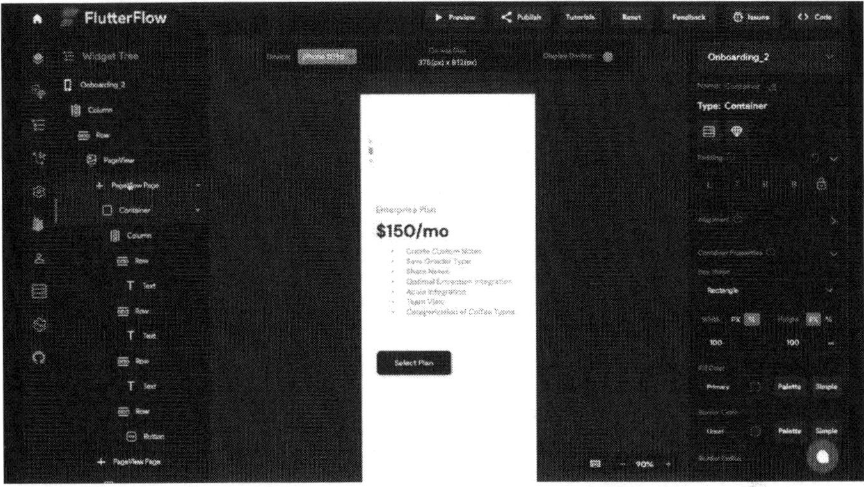

And now for the last page on our proposed scroll, we'll essentially repeat the processes for the first two designs. We'll copy that entire container in page two. You can also hex-code your container unit.

Now select the column and select **wrap**. Input your text and wrap it in a container. When you are done, copy the color used. Modify the size of your text if necessary. For the purpose of the demo, I'm not going to be too specific on the hex codes.

As a last step, be sure to save your project. When you view your saved project on FlutterFlow, you should be able to scroll through these three pages:

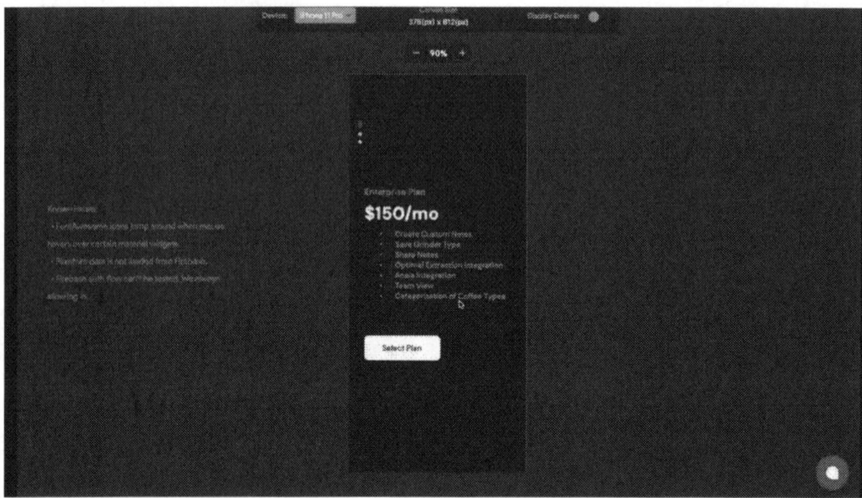

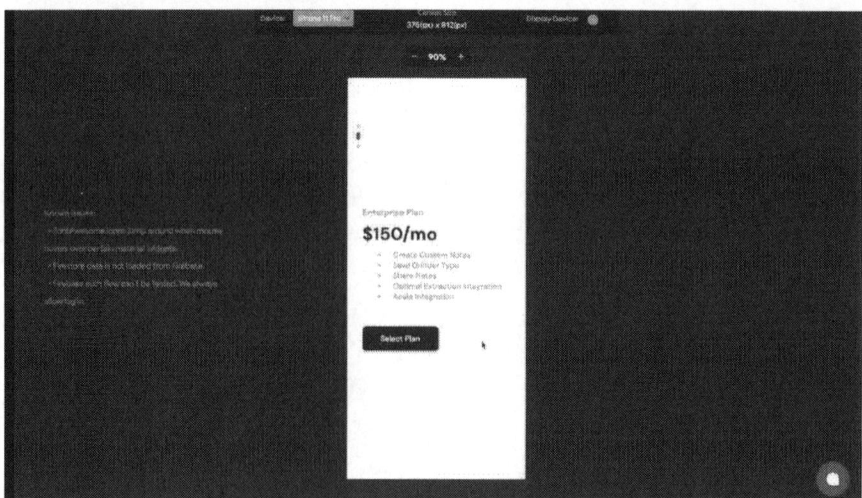

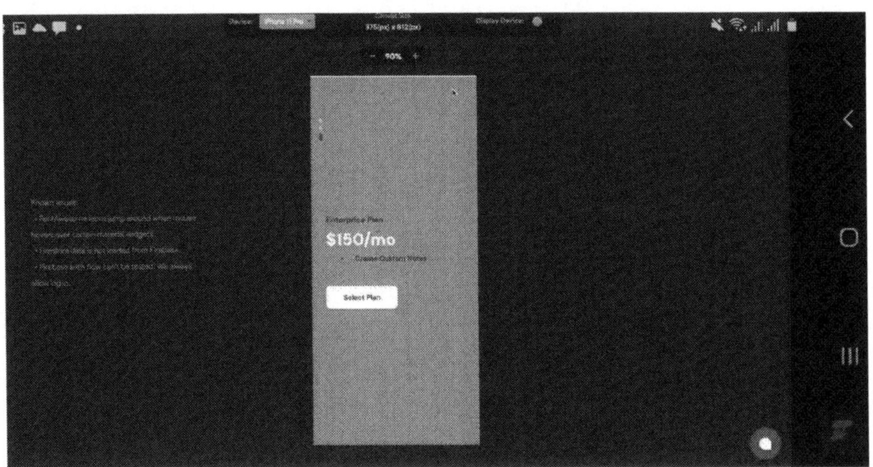

Conclusion

FlutterFlow is very easy to learn. You only need to learn the basic widgets and logic of Flutter. For everything else, like Firebase and Google Maps integration, there are tutorials from the official FlutterFlow YouTube channel. For more information on this sample project, please visit this link:

youtu.be/QGBKCUrZzJA

TWELVE

FlutterFlow Project 2 - Build a Chat App

Messaging apps are surging in popularity. These past few years have seen an influx of chat apps like WhatsApp. Today, more people seem to prefer chat-based applications, largely because these apps are so convenient. They allow for real-time interaction while simultaneously adding a personal touch to the experience. In this chapter, we'll explore how to add chats to your projects with FlutterFlow.

Prerequisite

Before you get started, make sure that you have Firebase already configured for your projects.

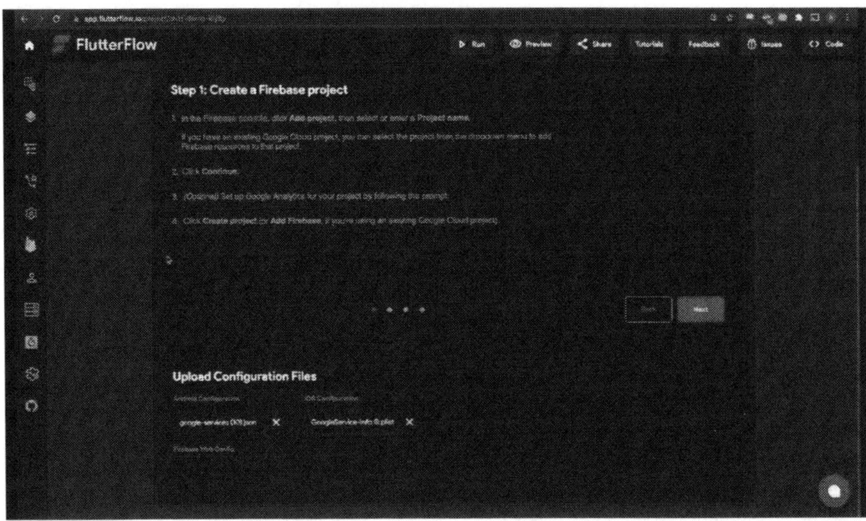

This means that you have to have your **config** files already added. You must already have set up authentication, so that you have your login page, homepage, and, of course, Firestore.

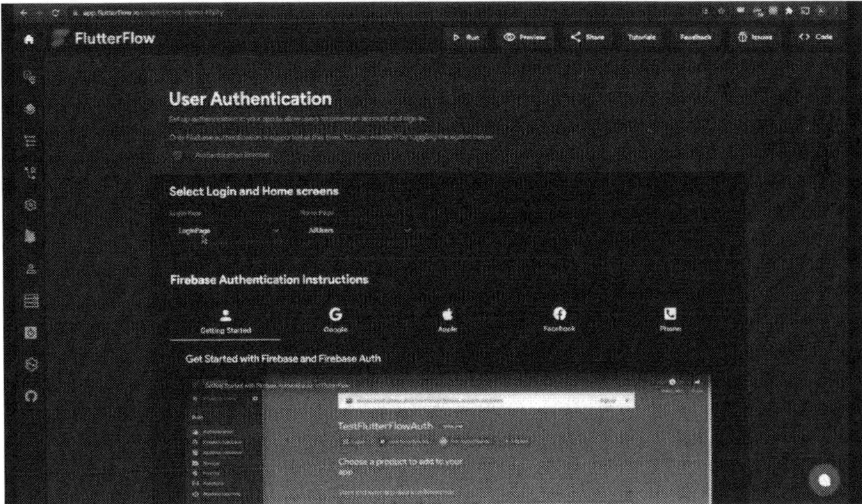

Also, you must have already defined your user's records and set up the **create user record**.

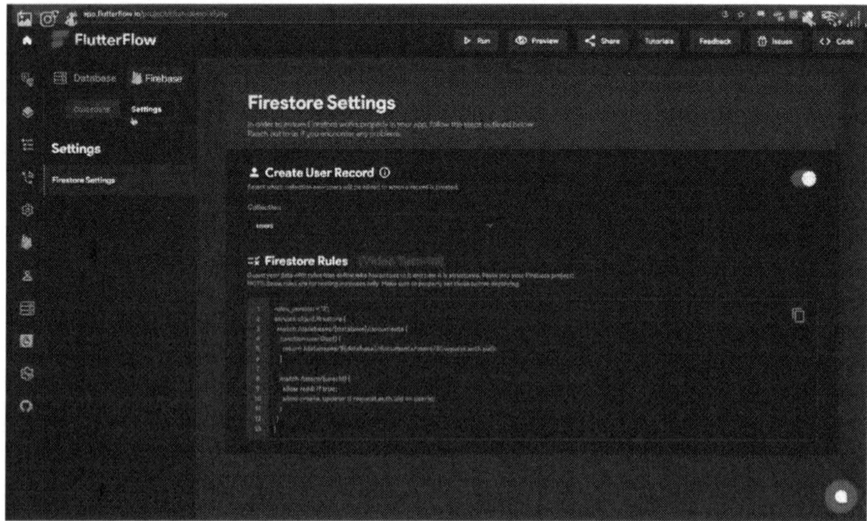

If your environment is not set up in this way, please refer to the information in the previous chapter to do so.

Now, as stated, our goal here is to add chats to our project using FlutterFlow, and we will start by creating a new page titled **chat page**.

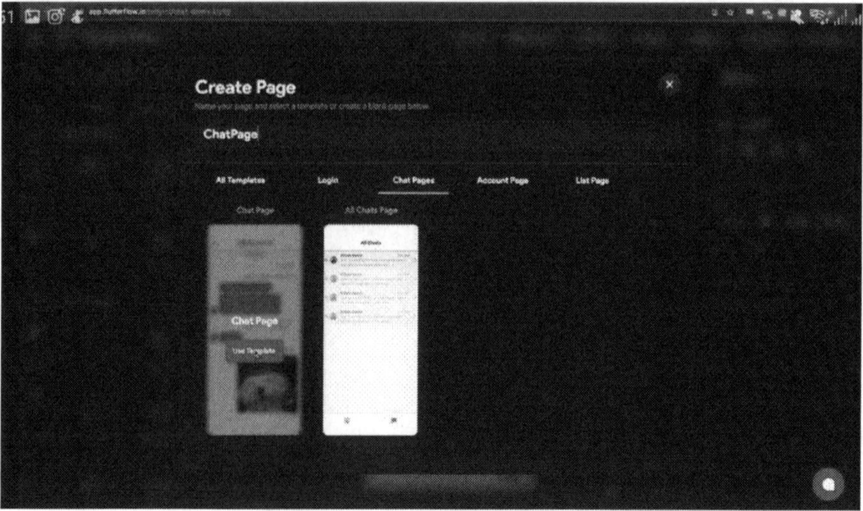

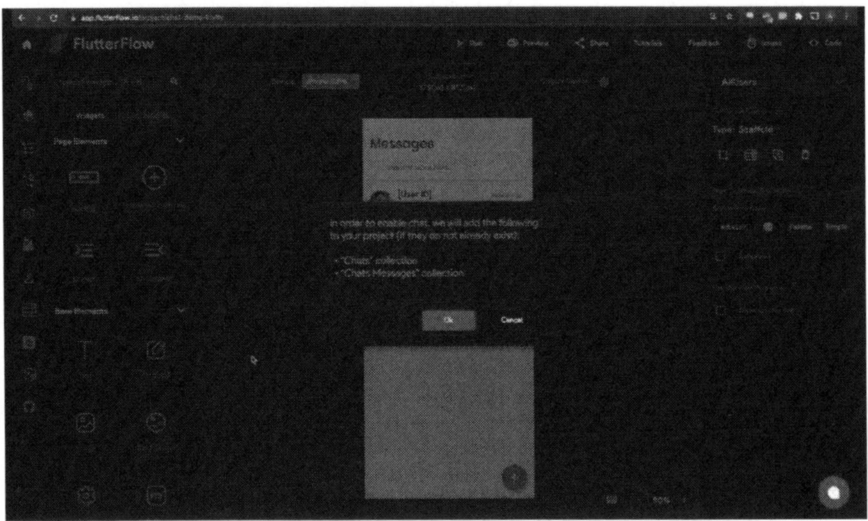

What this will do is automatically add the chat collection and your chat messages to your Firestore project.

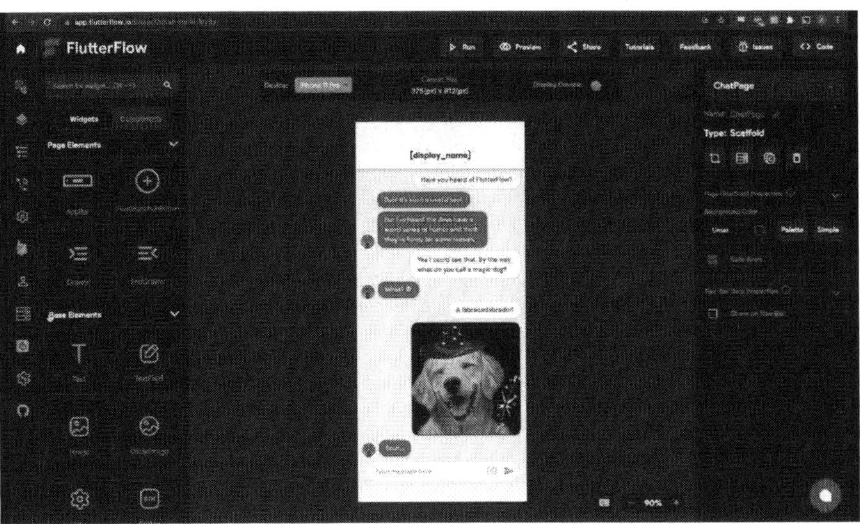

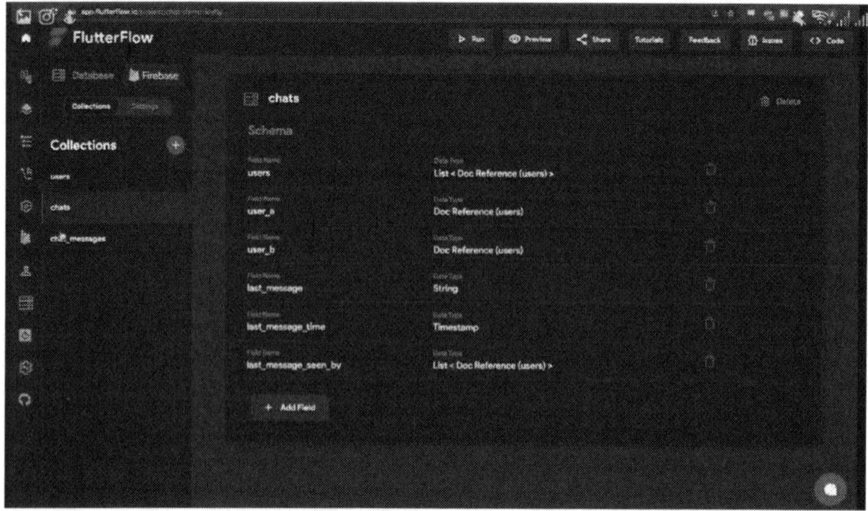

As you can see, we've added chats and chat messages. You don't need to change anything here. If you so choose, you can edit the colors to your liking. We can also go back and create a chat preview page, just to show all of our active chats.

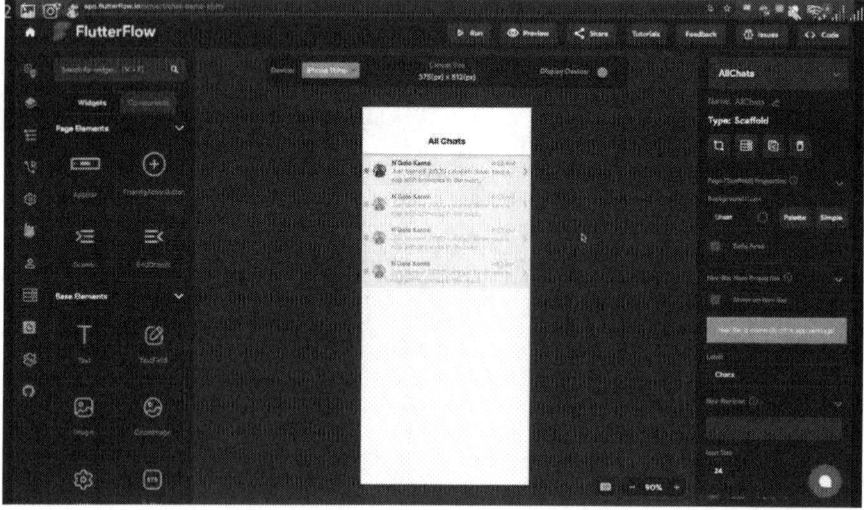

And again, there is no need to alter or modify this too much. This is merely a chat preview, and whether or not you choose to customize it, it shows all of your chats, most recent first. By the lower right-hand corner of your screen, you'll find the option to filter the chats you're in, so that they pop up in a decreasing time order.

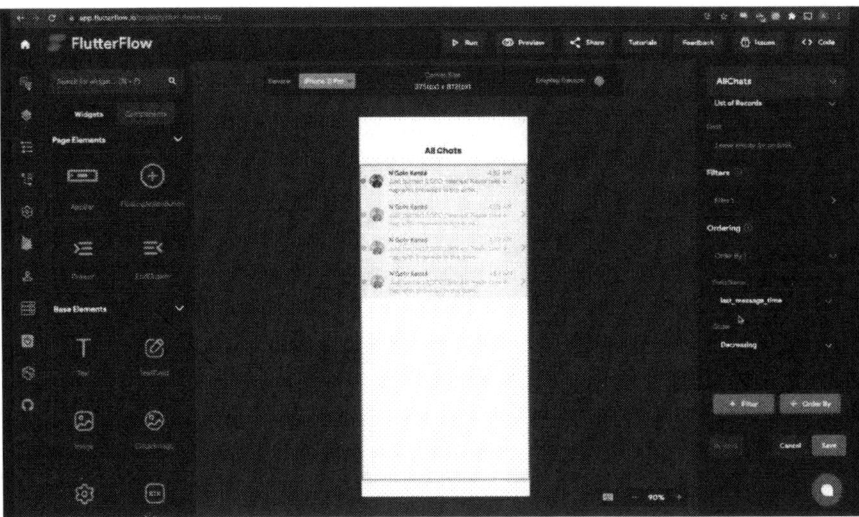

And that's really all there is to do here.

Now, the only other step is setting up the Firestore. Go to the Firestore tab, click on Settings, and you'll see the Firestore rules listed out.

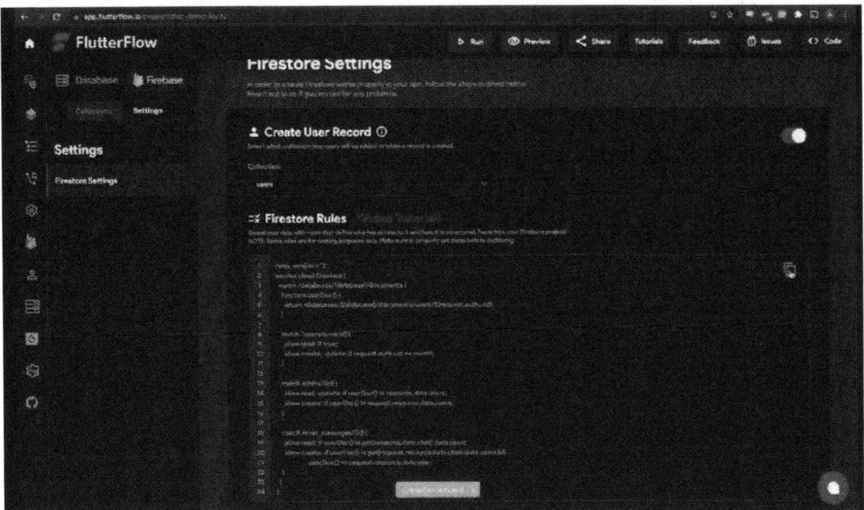

FlutterFlow has automatically created these security rules for users, and this works to make sure that only you and the people inside your chats can see the chats you're in. This is obviously important for security, so what we'll do here is copy these rules in our Firestore project and paste them here.

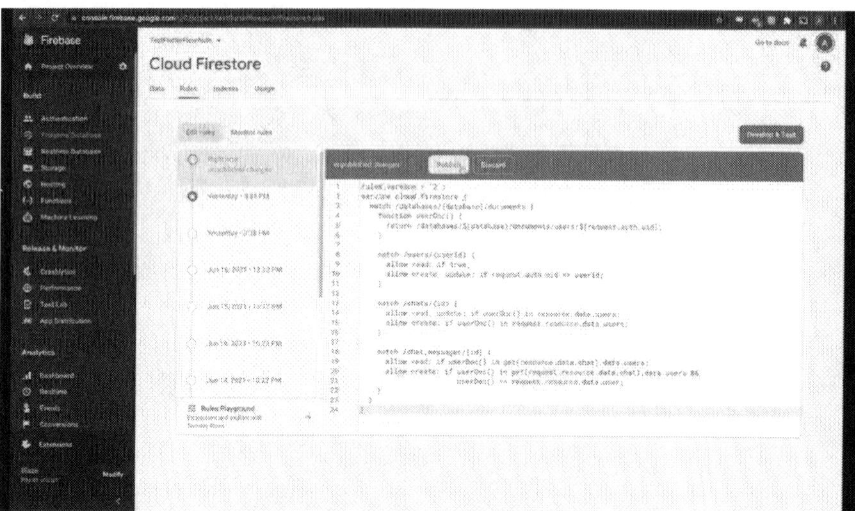

Once this is done, go ahead and click **Publish**. Now, one more important thing we need to do here is go to indexes.

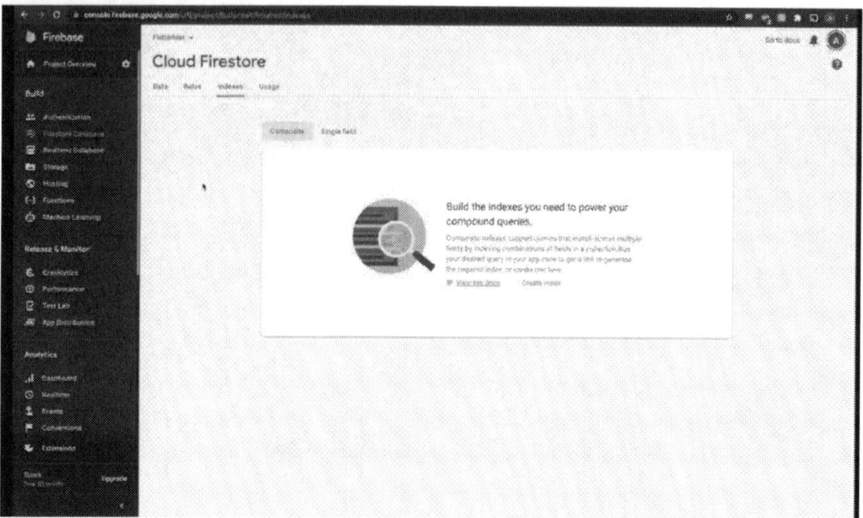

Indexes allow you to order and filter your data. For instance, you'll want the ability to filter chats by participant and sort by date. Same with chat messages: you need to make sure that the chat messages on your screen are the ones you are in, and also that the list is ordered so that the most recent chats are displayed at the bottom of the page. For this, we need to create two indexes.

Let's first create an index for chats, the first in our chats collection. Here ,we need to add users—that's an array. So, the chats collection has a users field, which is a list of the users that are in the chats—and you need to make sure that *you* are in the chat. That's why this field in the index is necessary.

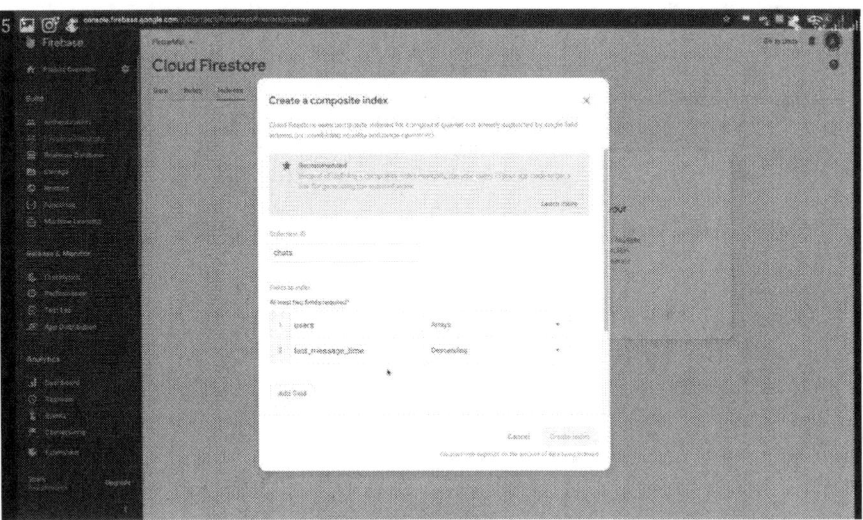

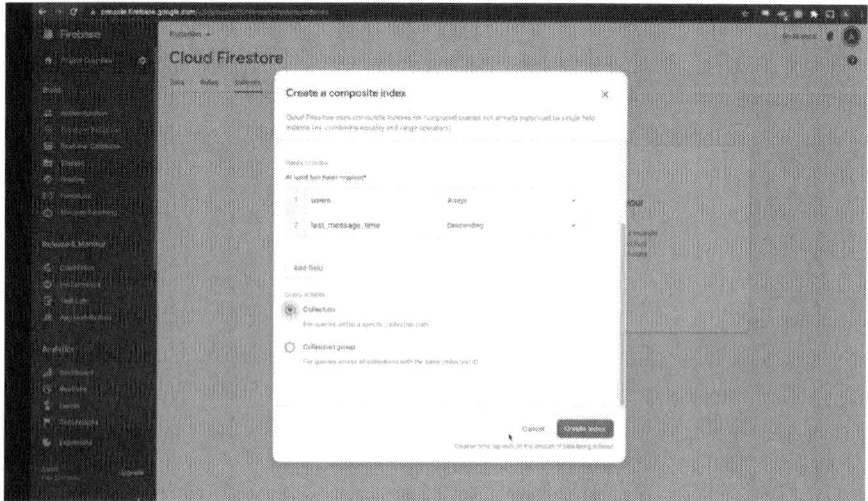

The other index field to work on is **last message time**, and we want to set it to descending order. Create this index not for a collection, but for a group.

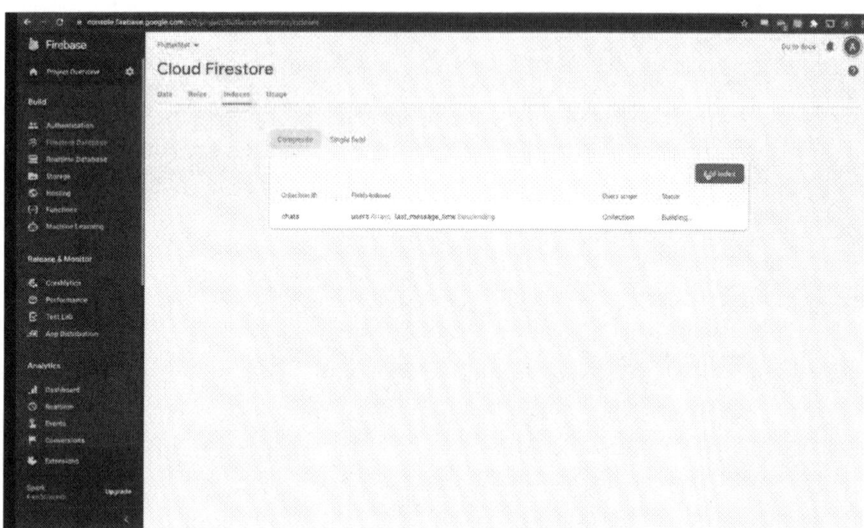

Now we'll do the same for chat messages. For this collection—chat messages—we'll add the chat field, because we want to make sure that our chat messages are parts of this particular chat and not some other chat. Again, we want to order by the most recent chat messages, so we'll order by timestamp, descending.

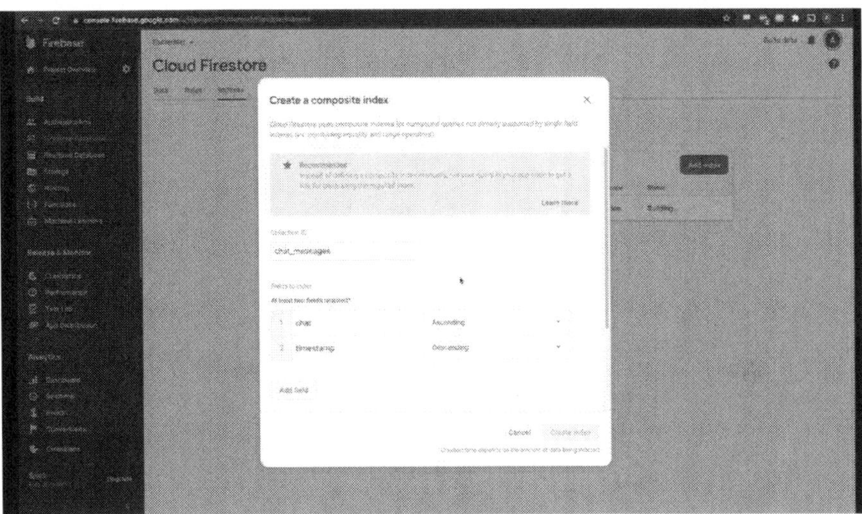

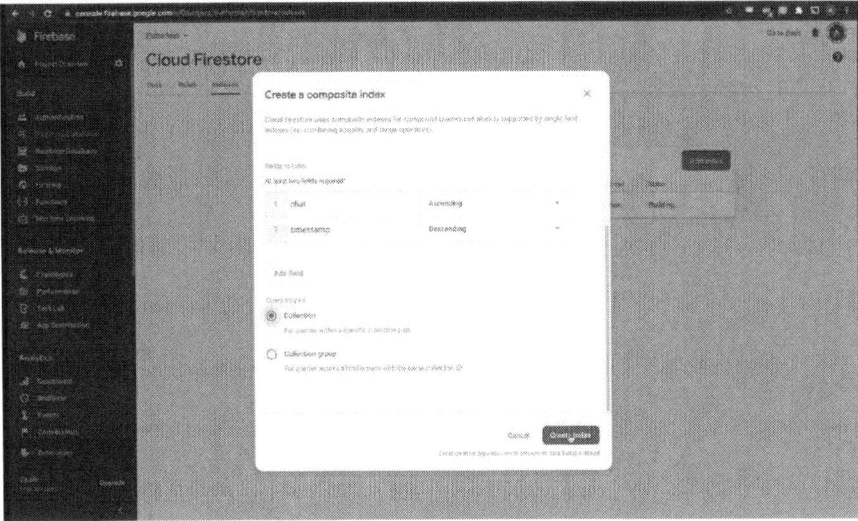

Here, select **collection → create index**, and we're done. We have a chat in our app, and we're ready to go.

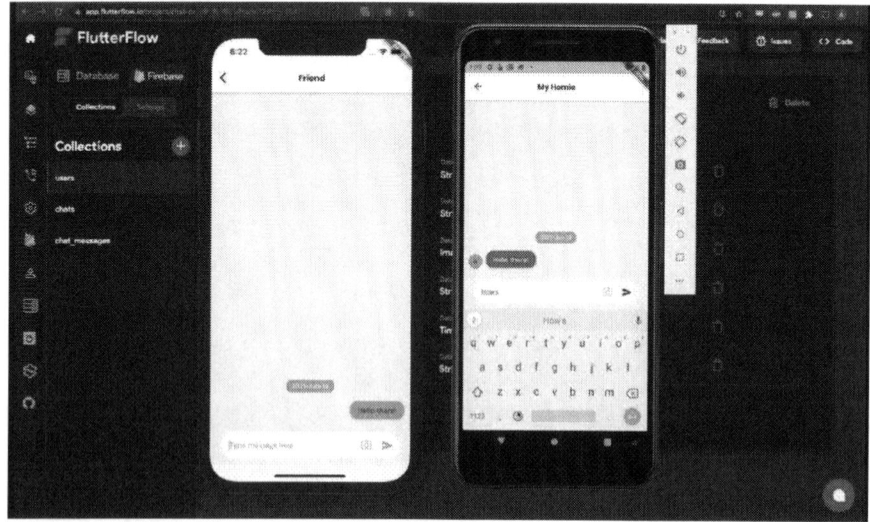

Conclusion

FlutterFlow is a relatively new app builder, but it is based on Flutter logic and works with the Flutter widgets. FlutterFlow uses certain packages to leverage their already built-in integrations, such as Google Maps. Also, FlutterFlow uses packages like **url_launcher**, **page_transition** or **intl**. By dragging and dropping, you can arrange widgets very quickly. To learn more about FlutterFlow, visit:

flutterflow.io.

THIRTEEN

Flutter and HTTP

Most Flutter projects entail **HTTP connectivity** between your app and a server-side API. The majority of the time, these server APIs follow the REST design rules, and data is sent in JSON format. The goal of this chapter is to teach you about HTTP before you start typing.

Asynchronous Communication

When your app uses HTTP to communicate with a remote server, it does so asynchronously. After sending a request to the server, the program does not abruptly halt. The Dart language, as you learned in Chapter Three, fully supports asynchronous programming, including Futures.

Futures are used by the Flutter HTTP package (which we shall explore shortly) to allow developers to communicate asynchronously over HTTP. We don't stop doing things in the app when we use HTTP to connect with the server; instead, we process the success or error answer as it comes back to us.

HTTP

The Hypertext Transfer Protocol (HTTP) is a protocol that allows clients and servers to communicate with each other. HTTP is a request-response protocol that communicates between a client and a server. A protocol explains how machines exchange messages with one another. The format of these communications is defined by a protocol.

Tools

Once you've mastered Flutter, you'll find yourself spending a lot of time creating code that interacts with servers through HTTP. I suggest you look into these tools ahead of time, because they will make your life easier. These are some of the tools available:

Web Browser

Obviously, you already own one of them. Open your browser, and go to a website. Now, utilize the hamburger menu to access the developer tools and observe the HTTP protocol in action. The network traffic inspector can be accessed by selecting the "network" option. The network traffic inspector may be seen on the right side of the image, with one request selected and inspected in greater detail.

Postman

Postman is an application programming interface (API) development tool that aids in the creation, testing, and modification of APIs. This utility contains almost all of the features that a developer would require. Before you code HTTP queries to a server in Flutter, you may use this tool to test them. You can see what's going on by looking at the raw data. Check it out here:

www.getpostman.com

JSON Formatter

The data format you'll be working with is in JSON format. To make the JSON more readable, you might want to look for a decent online JSON formatter. Check it out here:

jsonformatter.curiousconcept.com

Methods

HTTP methods have existed for quite some time. **POST**, **GET**, **PUT**, **PATCH**, and **DELETE** are the most often used HTTP methods. The method specifies what the app wants the server to do and what the request's goal is.

The methods **get** and **post** are the most regularly utilized. To request data from the server, use the **get** method. The **post** method is used to send, store, or update data to a server. To update data on the server, use the **put** method, and to delete data from the server, use the **delete** method.

URL

This is the destination address for the request, on a specific server and a certain path.

Query Parameters

Query parameters in HTTP allow you to pass information to the server in the URL. The main distinction is that query parameters apply to the entire request, whereas matrix parameters apply to a specific path element.

Matrix Parameters

Using matrix parameters, HTTP allows you to transmit information to the server in the URL. Matrix parameters have a similar structure to query strings, but they follow a distinct pattern. They also behave differently since they can be cached (due to the lack of a question mark).

Path Parameters

HTTP allows you to transmit information to the server using path parameters in the URL. Path parameters are used to identify a specific resource or resources, unlike query parameters, which are used to sort/filter resources. Because path parameters are part of the URL, you can't leave them blank.

Status

This is a part of the answer. It shows if the request was processed successfully or not.

Header

HTTP headers allow the client and server to provide additional data in the request or response. A request header is made up of key value pairs: a case-insensitive key, a colon (:), and then the value (without line breaks).

Body

After the header, the HTTP body allows the client and server to send additional information with the request or response.

Request

HTTP bodies are not always required in the request, because a body of data is not always necessary. A body is usually not required for **GET** and **DELETE** HTTP requests. The information to be created or edited is sent via **POST**, **PUT**, and **PATCH** HTTP requests.

Flutter and HTTP

We need to develop code that interfaces with APIs on servers using the HTTP protocol to convert data from Flutter to JSON and back. We'll utilize the Flutter HTTP Package to accomplish this. We'll have to add a dependency for this, because the Flutter HTTP is not a core package. Also, remember to execute a **flutter packages get**. More information is available here:

pub.dartlang.org/packages/http.

Error Handling

The Flutter HTTP package allows us to communicate with APIs asynchronously through HTTP, which complicates error handling:

- In the event that an error occurs during the request, you must add an error handler.
- In the event that the future stops with an error, you must include an error handler.
- Also, if an error occurs, you will have to check the HTTP code of the server's response to see if anything went wrong on their end.

Illustration

Let's create a sample Flutter app that uses the **http package** to perform HTTP requests to display placeholder information.

Prerequisites

This sample app presumes that:

- You have already downloaded and installed Flutter from flutter.dev/docs/get-started/install
- You have downloaded and installed either Android Studio from

developer.android.com/studio or Visual Studio Code from code.visualstudio.com

It is recommended that you also install plugins for your code editor:

- Flutter and Dart plugins for Android Studio. Get these from plugins.jetbrains.com/plugin/9212-flutter and plugins.jetbrains.com/plugin/6351-dart.
- Flutter extension for your Visual Studio Code. Get this from marketplace.visualstudio.com/items?itemName=Dart-Code.flutter.

1. Setting Up the Project

The first step is to set up the project. You'll be building a Flutter app to follow along with the setup. After you've set up your Flutter environment, use the following commands to build a new application:

```
flutter create flutter_http_example
```

Go to the following location to find the new project directory:

```
cd flutter_http_example
```

Through Flutter Create, you can make a demo app that shows how many times a button has been clicked. In your code editor, open **pubspec.yaml** and add the following plugin:

```
dependencies:

flutter:

sdk: flutter

http: ^0.12.0+2
```

This is an official Flutter plugin published by dart.dev here:

pub.dev/publishers/dart.dev/packages

It has a 100% health score, and you can trust the reliability of this plugin.

2. Handling GET Requests

The next step is to create a class that will allow you to interact with the API. Create a **http_service.dart** file in the **lib** directory with your code editor. You'll create a new **HttpService** class and add the **getPosts** function here:

lib/http_service.dart

```
import 'dart:convert';

import 'package:http/http.dart';
```

```
import 'post_model.dart';
class HttpService {
final String postsURL =
"https://jsonplaceholder.typicode.com/posts";
Future<List<Post>> getPosts() async {
Response res = await get(postsURL);
if (res.statusCode == 200) {
List<dynamic> body = jsonDecode(res.body);
List<Post> posts = body
.map(
(dynamic item) => Post.fromJson(item),
)
.toList();
return posts;
} else {
throw "Unable to retrieve posts.";
}
}
}
```

You'll be connecting to JSON Placeholder in this example. The **get** method of the http package is used on the **postsURL** string in this code. If the request was successful, this code will use **Post.fromJson** to return a **List<Post>**. Otherwise, an error message will be displayed.

Then, under the **lib** directory, create a **post_model.dart** file with your code editor. You will create a new **Post** class here:

```
import 'package:flutter/foundation.dart';
class Post {
final int userId;
final int id;
final String title;
final String body;
Post({
@required this.userId,
@required this.id,
@required this.title,
@required this.body,
});
factory Post.fromJson(Map<String, dynamic> json) {
return Post(
userId: json['userId'] as int,
id: json['id'] as int,
title: json['title'] as String,
body: json['body'] as String,
);
}
}
```

This code will return a new Post with the **fromJson** function based on a JSON Map in order to serialize the response from JSON Placeholder. JSON Placeholder typically returns a Post with a userId, id, title, and body.

3. Displaying Posts

After that, in the **lib** directory, create a **posts.dart** file with your code editor. Here, you'll make a **PostsPage** class that will show the Posts returned by the HTTP call to JSON Placeholder:

lib/posts.dart

```
import 'package:flutter/material.dart';
import 'http_service.dart';
import 'post_model.dart';
class PostsPage extends StatelessWidget {
final HttpService httpService = HttpService();
@override
Widget build(BuildContext context) {
return Scaffold(
appBar: AppBar(
title: Text("Posts"),
),
body: FutureBuilder(
future: httpService.getPosts(),
builder: (BuildContext context, AsyncSnapshot<List<Post>> snapshot) {
if (snapshot.hasData) {
List<Post> posts = snapshot.data;
return ListView(
children: posts
.map(
(Post post) => ListTile(
title: Text(post.title),
```

```
subtitle: Text("${post.userId}"),
),
)
.toList(),
);
} else {
return Center(child: CircularProgressIndicator());
}
},
),
);
}
}
```

The FutureBuilder widget is used to interact with the **getPosts()** function in this code. This enables the code to detect when the **List<Post>** is ready and take appropriate action. The **CircularProgressIndicator** is displayed if **snapshot.hasData** is false. Otherwise, the post information is shown in a **ListTile**. You'll need to replace the code in **main.dart** in order to see what you've got so far. Open your code editor and change **lib/main.dar**t to utilize **PostsPage**:

```
import 'package:flutter/material.dart';
import 'posts.dart';
void main() {
runApp(MyApp());
```

```
}
class MyApp extends StatelessWidget {
@override
Widget build(BuildContext context) {
return MaterialApp(
title: 'HTTP',
debugShowCheckedModeBanner: false,
theme: ThemeData(
primarySwatch: Colors.blue,
visualDensity: VisualDensity.adaptivePlatformDensity,
),
home: PostsPage(),
);
}
}
```

Compile and run your code in an emulator. JSON Placeholder should return a list of post titles and user ids to you. When a user clicks on a post title, the next step is to construct a comprehensive page with more information about the post.

4. Displaying PostDetail

Your app should redirect the user to a **PostDetail** page if the user taps on the post. Create a **post_detail.dart** file in the **lib** directory with your code editor. Here, you'll make a **PostDetail** class that will display a single Post:

lib/post_detail.dart

```
import 'package:flutter/material.dart';
import 'post_model.dart';
class PostDetail extends StatelessWidget {
final Post post;
PostDetail({@required this.post});

@override
Widget build(BuildContext context) {
return Scaffold(
appBar: AppBar(
title: Text(post.title),
),

body: SingleChildScrollView(
child: Padding(
padding: const EdgeInsets.all(12.0),
child: Column(
children: <Widget>[
Card(
child: Column(
crossAxisAlignment: CrossAxisAlignment.center,
children: <Widget>[
ListTile(
```

```
title: Text("Title"),
subtitle: Text(post.title),
),
ListTile(
title: Text("ID"),
subtitle: Text("${post.id}"),
),
ListTile(
title: Text("Body"),
subtitle: Text(post.body),
),
ListTile(
title: Text("User ID"),
subtitle: Text("${post.userId}"),
),
],
),
),
],
),
),
)
);
```

```
}
}
```

The title, id, body, and userId will all be displayed with this code. To see what you've got so far, you'll need to update **posts.dart** to include **post_detail.dart**:

lib/posts.dart

```
import 'package:flutter/material.dart';
import 'http_service.dart';
import 'post_detail.dart';
import 'post_model.dart';

class PostsPage extends StatelessWidget {
final HttpService httpService = HttpService();

@override
Widget build(BuildContext context) {
return Scaffold(
appBar: AppBar(
title: Text("Posts"),
),

body: FutureBuilder(
future: httpService.getPosts(),
```

```
builder: (BuildContext context, AsyncSnapshot<List<Post>>
snapshot) {
if (snapshot.hasData) {
List<Post> posts = snapshot.data;

return ListView(
children: posts

.map(
(Post post) => ListTile(
title: Text(post.title),
subtitle: Text("${post.userId}"),
onTap: () => Navigator.of(context).push(
MaterialPageRoute(

builder: (context) => PostDetail(
post: post,
),
),
),
),
)

.toList(),
);

} else {
return Center(child: CircularProgressIndicator());
```

```
}
},
),
);
}
}
```

Compile and test your code in an emulator. The final stage will be to include the option to delete a post.

5. Handling DELETE Requests

The **DELETE** method is an excellent example of an HTTP request. Create a **deletePost(int id)** method in **http_service.dart** in your code editor:

lib/http_service.dart

```
import 'dart:convert';
import 'package:http/http.dart';
import 'post_model.dart';

class HttpService {
final String postsURL = "https://jsonplaceholder.typicode.com/posts";

// ...
```

```
Future<void> deletePost(int id) async {
Response res = await delete("$postsURL/$id");

if (res.statusCode == 200) {
print("DELETED");
} else {
throw "Unable to delete post.";
}
}
}
```

In your code editor, go back to **post_detail.dart** and add an **IconButton** to the **actions array** within the AppBar. The corresponding post should be deleted when the icon is pressed:

```
import 'package:flutter/material.dart';
import 'http_service.dart';
import 'post_model.dart';

class PostDetail extends StatelessWidget {
final HttpService httpService = HttpService();
final Post post;
PostDetail({@required this.post});

@override
```

```
Widget build(BuildContext context) {

return Scaffold(
appBar: AppBar(
title: Text(post.title),
actions: <Widget>[
IconButton(
icon: Icon(Icons.delete),
onPressed: () async {
await httpService.deletePost(post.id);
Navigator.of(context).pop();
},
)
],
),
// ...
);
}
}
```

Compile and test your code in an emulator. The Delete icon button appears in the AppBar when you visit a post detail page. By pressing the button, a message will be printed in the console.

Output

flutter: DELETED

This is a request to delete items. This post will not be erased, however, due to the constraints of JSON Placeholder and this example application.

Conclusion

You learned how to use the Flutter http package in this chapter. You may **GET** a list of posts and **DELETE** a single post using this method. Post, place, patch, and other similar procedures are also accessible. For more information, check out the official documentation here:

pub.dev/documentation/http/latest/

FOURTEEN

Debugging

The goal of this chapter is to assist you with debugging, diagnosing, and profiling your Flutter projects. Flutter provides us with fantastic tools to make debugging easier, supplying uswith any information we might need. This is a vast topic, and all this chapter can do is "dip its toe in the water." I'll show you how to use Debugging In Flutter, as well as define its properties and use them in your Flutter apps.

Flutter Debugging

Flutter provides a variety of devices and capabilities to aid with the debugging of applications. The equipment and facilities listed below are on display.

- **DevTools:** The go-to tool for debugging apps may be DevTools. It's a browser-based set of performance and profiling tools.
- **Logging:** Logging view widget Inspector in DevTools, as well as indirectly from Android Studio and IntelliJ IDEA. The widget tree visual representation can be checked using the inspector.

- **Debug Flags:** Debug Flags gives us a choice of debug flags and functions to help us debug our program at different moments. You must compile in debug mode, though, in order to use these functionalities.

Code Implement

The debug flag and some of its functions will be discussed here. These include **debugPaintSizeEnabled**, **debugPaintBaselineEnabled**, **debugPaintLayerBorderEnabled** and **debugRepaintRainbow-Enabled**.

To begin, we need to first import **rendering.dart** from Flutter.

```
import 'package:flutter/rendering.dart';
```

debugPaintSizeEnabled

This screen makes use of the type's **paint size embed** feature. It generates a render box around the screen and highlights it with several colors and a thick line on the side. Let's demonstrate this with a simple example:

```
debugPaintSizeEnabled = true;
```

When the app is debugged, we should be able to see the screen output, as shown in the snapshot below.

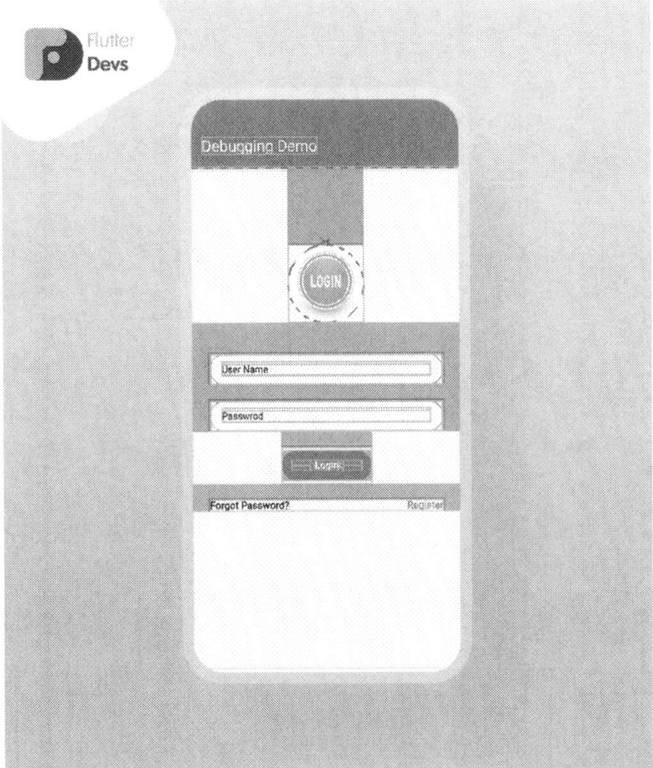

debugPaintBaselineEnabled

This flag paints a line on each baseline in the screen. Now add **debugPaintBaselineEnabled= true** in the main function to illustrate this further:

```
debugPaintBaselinesEnabled = true;
```

When the app is debugged through this means, we should be able to see the screen output, as shown in the image below.

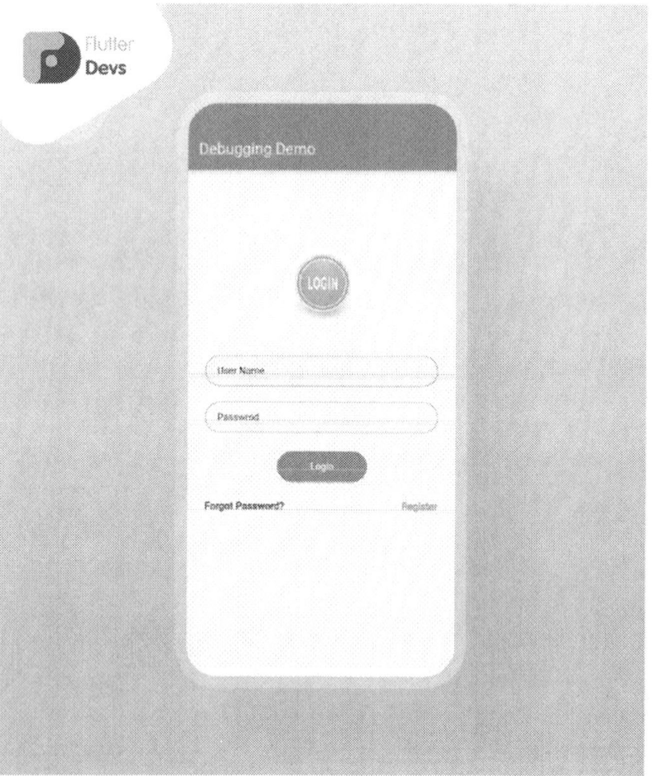

debugPaintLayerBorderEnabled

This generates a paint line and turns each layer in the screen into a box with a boundary. When you add **debugPaintLayerBordersEnabled**, restart the app.

```
debugPaintLayerBordersEnabled = true;
```

When the app is debugged, we should be able to see the screen output, as shown in the snapshot below.

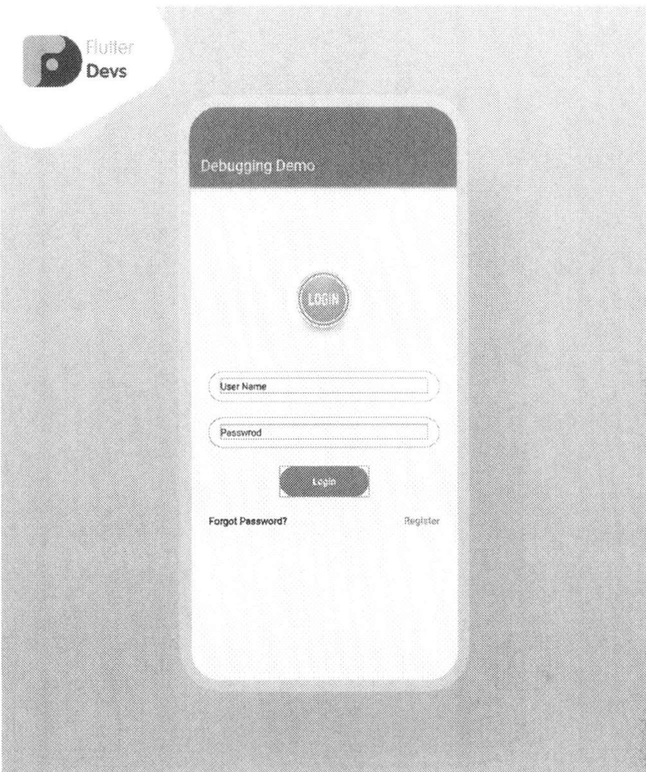

debugRepaintRainbowEnabled

When repeating layers in checked mode after running in debug mode on the screen, this overlays the revolving set of colors.

```
debugRepaintRainbowEnabled = true;
```

When the app is debugged, we should be able to see the screen output, as shown in the snapshot below.

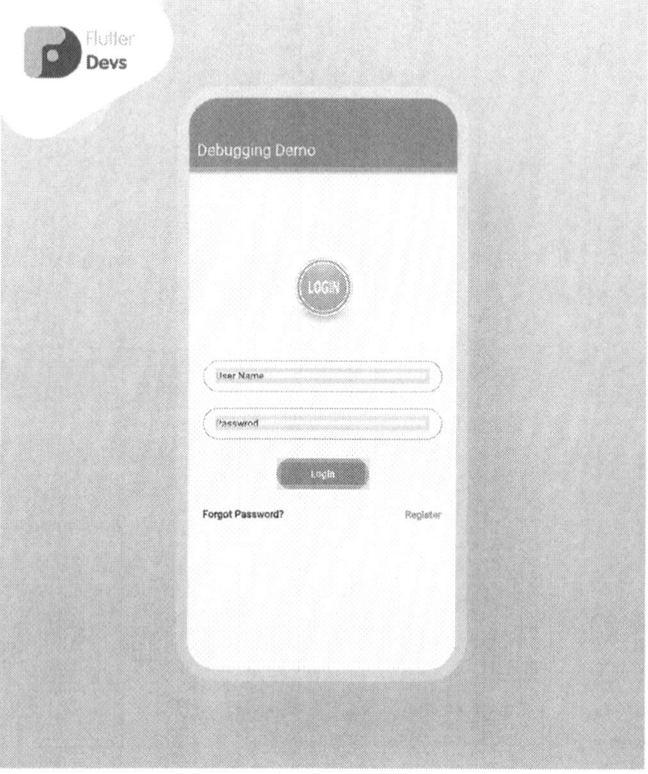

```
import 'package:flutter/material.dart';

import
'package:flutter_debugging_demo/shared/custom_button.dart';

import
'package:flutter_debugging_demo/shared/custom_text_field.dart';

import
'package:flutter_debugging_demo/themes/appthemes.dart';
```

```
import
'package:flutter_debugging_demo/themes/device_size.dart';

import 'package:flutter/rendering.dart';

class DebuggingDemo extends StatefulWidget {

@override

_DebuggingDemoState createState() =>

_DebuggingDemoState();

}

class _DebuggingDemoState extends State<DebuggingDemo> {

@override

Widget build(BuildContext context) {

debugPaintSizeEnabled = true;

debugPaintBaselinesEnabled = false;

debugPaintLayerBordersEnabled = false;

debugRepaintRainbowEnabled = false;

debugRepaintTextRainbowEnabled = false;

debugCheckElevationsEnabled = false;

debugDisableClipLayers = false;

debugDisablePhysicalShapeLayers = false;

debugDisableOpacityLayers = false;

return Scaffold(

appBar: AppBar(

title: Text('Debugging Demo'),

),
```

```
body: Container(
height: DeviceSize.height(context),
width: DeviceSize.width(context),
child: Column(
children: [
Container(
margin: EdgeInsets.only(top: 100),
//alignment:Alignment.bottomCenter,
child: ClipOval(
child: CircleAvatar(
backgroundColor: Colors.transparent,
maxRadius: 50,
child: Image.asset(
'assets/images/login.jpeg',
fit: BoxFit.cover,
width: DeviceSize.width(context),
),
),
),
),
Container(
padding: EdgeInsets.only(top: 40, left: 25, right: 25),
child: CustomTextField(
hintText: 'User Name',
```

```
type: TextInputType.text,
obscureText: false,
labelText: '',
),
),
Container(
padding: EdgeInsets.only(top: 20, left: 25, right: 25),
child: CustomTextField(
hintText: 'Password',
type: TextInputType.text,
obscureText: true,
labelText: '',
),
),
Container(
margin: EdgeInsets.only(top: 20),
child: CustomButton(
callbackTertiary: () {
debugDumpApp();
},
color: Colors.blue,
mainButtonText: 'Login',
),
),
```

```
Container(
padding: EdgeInsets.only(top: 20, left: 25, right: 25),
child: Row(
mainAxisAlignment: MainAxisAlignment.spaceBetween,
children: [
Text(
'Forgot Password?',
style: TextStyle(fontSize: 13, fontWeight: FontWeight.w700),
),
Text(
'Register',
style: TextStyle(
color: Colors.blue,
fontSize: 13,
fontWeight: FontWeight.w700),
),
],
),
),
],
),
),
);
}
```

```
void debugDumpApp() {
assert(WidgetsBinding.instance != null);
String mode = 'RELEASE MODE';
assert(() {
mode = 'CHECKED MODE';
return true;
}());
debugPrint('${WidgetsBinding.instance.runtimeType} - $mode');
if (WidgetsBinding.instance.renderViewElement != null) {
debugPrint(WidgetsBinding.instance.renderViewElement.toStringDeep());
} else {
debugPrint('<no tree currently mounted>');
}
}
}
```

Debugging Tools

There are a wide variety of tools and features to help debug Flutter applications.

The Dart Analyzer

Flutter Analyze helps you test your code before you run it. This tool is a wrapper for the dartanalyzer tool, which really analyzes your code and assists you in finding potential errors. The Dart analyzer makes extensive use of type annotations, which you can provide in your code to aid in the detection of errors. You should use them everywhere, because it is the quickest and easiest method to trace down errors—but avoid var, untyped arguments, untyped list literals, and so on.

Dart Observatory (Statement-level Single-stepping Debugger and Profiler)

If you use Flutter Run to start your app, you may open the web page at the observatory URL printed to the console while it's running. Profiling, analyzing the heap, and other tasks are also supported by the Dart Observatory. The Observatory's documentation has more information:

dart-lang.github.io/observatory

If you're profiling your app with Observatory, make sure to run it in profile mode by supplying **—profile** to the **flutter run** command. You may also use the built-in debugger in a Flutter-enabled IDE/editor to debug your application.

Debugger() Statement

You can add temporary code to detect a condition and start the debugger when you're troubleshooting to try and reproduce it. Flutter allows you to use your IDE's debugger directly from your code using this sentence. This is equivalent to the debugger statement for JavaScript.

Keep in mind to import **dart:developer** at the beginning. The **debugger()** instruction can be used to introduce programmatic breakpoints when using the Dart Observatory (or another Dart debugger integrated into a Flutter capable IDE/editor). To use it, add **import 'dart:developer'**; to the start of your file. When you use the d**ebugger()** command, you can give an optional **when** parameter to only break when a certain condition is true, like in:

```
void someFunction(double offset) {
debugger(when: offset > 30.0);
// ...
}
```

Print and debugPrint with Flutter Logs

The Dart **print()** function prints to the system console, which you can inspect with the Flutter **logs** command (which is basically a wrapper around adb logcat). When you produce a large amount of data at once, Android may discard some log lines. To avoid this, utilize Flutter's foundation library's **debugPrint()** method. This is a wrapper for **print** that compresses the output to a level that avoids the kernel of Android dropping it.

Many of the Flutter framework's classes have **toString** implementations, and these are handy. They usually emit a single line with the object's **runtimeType**, which is commonly in the form **ClassName**. **ToStringDeep** is a method in some tree classes that returns a multiline description of the complete subtree from that point. Some classes include a **toStringShort** method that returns simply the type or a very brief (one or two word) description of the object, which is useful if the toString implementation is very verbose.

Debug mode assertions

Using Flutter's **debug mode** while development is highly recommended. If you use **flutter run** or the bug icon in Android Studio, this is the default. The command line argument **—enable-asserts** is used by some utilities to support assert statements.

The Flutter framework examines the argument to each assert statement encountered during execution in this mode, throwing an exception if the result is false and if Dart assert statements are enabled. This allows developers to enable or disable invariant testing, and the performance cost associated with it is only paid during debugging sessions.

When an invariant is broken, it is sent to the console along with additional context information to aid in the investigation of the problem. To utilize release mode instead of debug mode, run your app with **flutter run —release**. This would also turn the Observatory debugger off.

An intermediate mode, known as "profile mode," is also available, which disables all debugging aids except the Observatory and uses —**profile** instead of **—release**.

For more information, see Flutter's modes here:

lutter.axuer.com/docs/testing/build-modes

Conclusion

I've explained debugging in Flutter in this chapter, providing examples that you can modify and experiment with on your own. Even though this brief introduction was taken from Flutter's Debugging demo, please try it out on your own Flutter project applications. There is only so much we can cover in this chapter. I encourage you check out more information here:

medium.com/flutterdevs

FIFTEEN

Other Considerations

This chapter serves "hook" for anything else you should think about when creating your software with Flutter. This is important, because aside from the creation of your project and its development into an app, there are some final points to double check before you publish your app.

HTTP Communication

While we have discussed Flutter and the HTTP package previously, it is important that before we go into further detail on Flutter speed, we reiterate that most Flutter apps will interact with other computers. Considering that network connectivity is generally substantially slower than the Flutter user interface, examining how your app connects with other computers is a smart place to start and can produce considerable benefits.

Data Considerations

It's critical to understand what data each server sends you, because you might not need them all. Do you require all of the data elements? Is there any way to reduce the size of the data? Is it possible to save some of the data in a cache and only refresh the cache once in a while? Is it possible to submit many requests to the server and have them all execute asynchronously at the same time? The more answers you have here, the smoother your work will be.

Avoid Rebuilding All the Widgets Repetitively

We learn to rebuild our stateful widgets using **setState**, which is a common mistake we make when we first start using Flutter. It is not good practice to rebuild the entire widget; instead, we should rebuild only the parts that need to be updated.

Many people are aware that this may be accomplished using a state management package such as flutter bloc, mobx, provider, and so on. Few people realize, however, that it can be done without any extra packages, using classes that the Flutter framework already includes, such as **ValueNofifier** and **changeNofifier**.

Isolates

Dart executes in a single thread. This sounds fantastic, until you realize you'll have to do a lot of heavy processing. When you perform all your processes on a single thread, the intensive processing prevents your user interface from updating and makes it sluggish.

With **Isolates**, you can execute massive processing while keeping the user interface current and responsive. Dart's version of a thread is an isolate. Isolates, unlike threads, do not share memory with other processes and communicate with each other via messages and ports. You can send a message from the isolation to the main thread to update the UI (for example, the progress bar), and it will update immediately.

Use Const Widgets Where Possible

For constants that can be initialized at compile time, it's best to use the keyword **const**. Let's not forget to use const for our widgets as much as is feasible; this allows us to capture and reuse widgets, avoiding costly rebuilds.

Use the **const** keyword to avoid possible instantiation/rebuilds when utilizing stateless widgets. Constants also save memory, since, no matter how many times the **const** expression(s) are evaluated, a single **const** object will be constructed and reused for each given const value.

Use itemExtent in ListView for Long Lists

The use of **itemExtent** is quite significant when you have a really long list and want to make a sharp jump with the scroll. In a long list, if we ignore the **itemExtent** in **ListView** and let the children define the size of the list, the jump would be quite slow at 10 seconds. This can make our work more challenging—it even disables the user interface.

To avoid this, we can use the **itemExtent** property, which allows the scrolling machinery to save time by taking advantage of the foreknowledge of the children's extent.

Avoid Rebuilding Unnecessary Widgets inside AnimatedBuilder

Adding animation to our widgets is a common request. We usually add a listener to our **AnimationController** and call **setState** from there. However, this isn't always a good idea.

Instead, we'll utilize the **AnimatedBuilder** widget to only rebuild the widget we wish to animate. It is recreating your widget while rotating. If you have a lot of print statements, you can use the **AnimatedBuilder**'s child attribute, which allows you to cache widgets and reuse them in your animation. We do this because the widget will not change; the only thing it will do is rotate, which the Transform widget can handle.

Use Finals Whenever Possible

This improves not only efficiency, but readability, as well, because you know the value of that instance variable is unchangeable. If you have instance variables that are only set in the constructor, for example, you can mark them as final.

Conclusion

Even though Flutter is powerful enough to run our apps without problems, it is always good to follow best practices and optimize your app as much as possible. You can check out these links for more helpful information:

https://api.flutter.dev/flutter/widgets/StatefulWidget-class.html#performance-considerations

https://flutter.dev/docs/perf/rendering/best-practices

SIXTEEN

Publishing Your App

The process of making your mobile applications available to users is known as **publishing**. When you publish a mobile app, you have two major steps to complete:

- You finish the application and get it ready for release. You create a release version of your software during the preparation stage, which people may download and install on their devices.
- You release the app to users. You market, sell, and distribute the release version of your application to users during the release process.

I'll give you an overview of the steps you should take as you prepare to publish your app here. This chapter's goal is to serve as a "catch-all" for anything connected to publishing your Flutter app.

How to Release Your Flutter App for iOS

Prerequisites

- Check to see if you've followed Apple's requirements for publishing an app on the App Store.
- Prepare the icons and launch screens for your app.
- Have a developer account with Apple.

Get Ready to Build

You must first set up an App Store Connect account before you can build and release your app on the App Store. To do this, you should first register a unique bundle ID for your app. This can be done when you login to your Apple Developer account, following the instructions below:

- Navigate to the **App IDs** page.
- To create a new Bundle ID, click **+**.
- Fill in the required fields: App Name and Explicit App ID.
- Select the services that your app requires and click **Continue**.
- To finish, review the information and click **Register**.

Now that we have a unique bundle ID, it's time to create a Project Store Connect account for your app. Connect to the App Store by logging in.

- Choose **My Apps**.
- Select **New App** after clicking **+**.
- After filling in your app's details and ensuring that iOS is selected, click **Create**.
- Select **App Information** from the sidebar.
- Select the Bundle ID that you registered above in the **General Information** section.

Adjust Xcode Project Settings for Release

You've completed Apple's setup, and now you'll tweak your Xcode project's settings to get your app ready for release. Start Xcode and see what you can come up with.

- Open the **Runner.xcworkspace** file in the iOS folder of your project.
- Select the **Runner** project from the Xcode project navigator.
- Then, in the main view sidebar, select the **Runner** target.
- Click on the **General** tab.
- Fill in the details in the **Identity** area, making sure the **Bundle Identifier** matches the one registered on App Store Connect.
- Make sure that **Automatically manage signing** is checked in the **Signing** section, and then select your team.
- Complete the remaining fields as needed.
- After that, you'll change the icon for your app by selecting **Assets.xcassets** in the **Runner** folder from Xcode's project navigator.

Build and Upload Your App

Now, all of your settings have been modified for release, and a placeholder has been created on App Store Connect, allowing you to build and release.

- Run **flutter build ios** from the command line.
- Return to Xcode and restart **Runner.xcworkspace**.
- Choose **Product → Scheme → Runner**.
- Also click on **Product → Destination → Generic iOS Device**.
- To create a build archive, go to **Product → Archive**.
- Select your iOS app from the sidebar in the Xcode Organizer window, then select the build archive you just created.

- To build, click the **Validate** button.
- Click **Upload to App Store** after the archive has been successfully authenticated.

Return to App Store Connect and check the Activities tab to see how your build is doing. When it's all set to release:

- Fill out the needed information under **Pricing and Availability**.
- Select the **Status** from the sidebar.
- Select **Prepare for Submission** and fill out all of the fields that are required.
- Finally, click on **Submit for Review**.

Your app will now be successfully posted to the App Store. Apple will review or evaluate your app before it is released, but they will keep you informed about its progress at all times.

How to Release Your Flutter App for Android

Prerequisites

- Make sure you have an Android app ready to go.
- Create a launcher icon and gather all of your app's assets.

Prepare for Release

A digital signature is required before your Flutter app can be published on Google Play. Create a **keystore** if you don't already have one on Mac with the following command:

```
keytool -genkey -v -keystore ~/key.jks -keyalg RSA -keysize 2048 -
validity 10000 -alias key
```

Use the following command on Windows:

```
keytool -genkey -v -keystore c:/Users/USER_NAME/key.jks -
storetype JKS -keyalg RSA -keysize 2048 -validity 10000
-alias key
```

Add a file called **/android/key.properties** that references your keystore. It should look like this:

```
storePassword= keyPassword= keyAlias=key

storeFile=/key.jks>
```

Configure Signing in Gradle

Your Gradle file is located at **/android/app/build.gradle**. Begin editing by going through the following steps.

Replace . . .

```
android {
```

. . . with the keystore information that we just created, as seen below:

```
def keystoreProperties = new Properties()

def keystorePropertiesFile = rootProject.file('key.properties')

if (keystorePropertiesFile.exists()) {

keystoreProperties.load(new
FileInputStream(keystorePropertiesFile))

}

android {
```

Then, also replace the following. . .

```
content_copy

buildTypes {

release {
```

```
// TODO: Add your own signing config for the release build.
// Signing with the debug keys for now,
// so `flutter run --release` works.
signingConfig signingConfigs.debug
}
}
```

. . . with the signing configuration info:

```
content_copy
signingConfigs {
release {
keyAlias keystoreProperties['keyAlias']
keyPassword keystoreProperties['keyPassword']
storeFile keystoreProperties['storeFile'] ?
file(keystoreProperties['storeFile']) : null
storePassword keystoreProperties['storePassword']
}
}
buildTypes {
release {
signingConfig signingConfigs.release
```

```
}
}
```

After that, navigate to the **defaultConfig** block and:

- Create a final **applicationId** that is unique.
- Give your app a **versionName** and a **versionCode**.
- Set the minimum SDK API level required for the app to run.

Your app's Gradle file is now configured, and your release builds will be signed automatically. Examine the app manifest closely, so as to ensure that everything is in working order. In addition, the file **AndroidManifest.xml** can be found in the **/android/app/src/main** directory. Before you start building, open this and go over the values and permissions you'll need.

Build and Release the App

Now you'll create the APK for your program, which will be posted to the Google Play Store. To get started, go to your command prompt and type the following commands:

- Enter **cd**
- Then **run flutter build apk**

Exempting any errors, an APK will be accessible at this point in **/build/app/outputs/apk/release/app.apk**. Your app is now ready to be published on the Google Play store. For further reading, visit:

https://flutter.dev/docs/deployment/android

https://flutter.dev/docs/deployment/ios

Final Words

Flutter is exceptional for very many reasons. If you are new to mobile development, Flutter will give you a fast, fun and modern way to deliver native apps. If you are a more experienced mobile developer, you can add Flutter to your existing workflow and tools to build new expressive UIs.

We'll conclude this journey with a summary of all that we looked at in this book:

- **Basic Terminologies:** An understanding of these basic concepts is necessary for you before you delve into the world of Flutter.
- **Introduction To Dart:** Dart is an object-oriented programming language designed for client development, indispensable to Flutter applications. We looked at some advanced Dart Samples to illustrate how the language functions.
- **Introduction To Flutter:** We looked at the core components of Flutter, Google's open-source SDK for creating apps for Android and iOS using a single codebase. We reviewed all the ways it's simpler than React Native and went further to discuss

its latest version: Flutter 2.2. We also worked on five different flutter projects in this book. and I hope you grasped enough to attempt to develop some of yours.

- **Project Using FlutterFlow:** We reviewed two sample projects with FlutterFlow, and while there are many more, the idea here was to provide you with a foundational understanding of how this software works.
- **Flutter and HTTP:** Flutter provides an http package that supports making HTTP requests. HTTP has tools like Response, Request, Postman and JSON Formatter alongside its methods such as POST, GET, or DELETE—all to ensure a smoother communication. The Flutter HTTP package uses Futures to enable developers to communicate through HTTP asynchronously, as we demonstrated this in the book.
- **Debugging:** Flutter provides multiple debugging tools, such as timeline inspector, memory and performance inspector, and more. These tools ease up the debugging process for a developer. We also implemented a demo of Debugging In Flutter, describing its properties and how to use them in your Flutter applications.
- **Publishing Your App:** We rounded up by discussing other final considerations and how to deploy your Flutter app on the App Store and Google Play.

Thank you for coming along on this journey. The author of this book wishes you a long, happy, and purposeful life.

References

Without the materials and sources listed below, I would not have been able to complete even 10% of this book. For this reason, I am grateful to everyone who contributed to these sources in any way, including:

Those contributing to the Flutter Dev group on Google: https://groups.google.com/forum/

Those contributing to the Medium flutter community: https://medium.com/flutter-community

Official Resources

The official Flutter website can be found at http://flutter.io/. In case you want an offline copy, the source code is here: https://github.com/flutter/website. You can clone the repository. This is great if you sometimes have to work without an internet connection.

"Cookbook." Flutter.dev. Accessed July 2021. https://flutter.dev/docs/cookbook.

"Dart2Native Tools." Dart.cn. Accessed July 2021. https://dart.cn/tools/dart2native.

"Dart Overview." Dart.dev. Accessed July 2021. https://dart.dev/overview.

"Debugging Flutter Apps." Flutter.dev. Accessed July 2021. https://flutter.dev/docs/testing/debugging.

"Flutter Build Release Channels." GitHub. Accessed July 2021. https://github.com/flutter/flutter/wiki/Flutter-build-release-channels.

Flutter by Example. Accessed July 2021. https://flutterbyexample.com.

"Flutter Widget Index." Accessed July 2021. https://flutter.dev/docs/reference/widgets.

FlutterFlow. Accessed July 2021. https://flutterflow.io.

"FlutterFlow Official Channel." YouTube. Accessed July 2021. https://youtube.com/channel/UC5LueiosDVInA6yXE_38i9Q

"Google Developers' Channel." YouTube. Accessed July 2021. https://www.youtube.com/channel/UC_x5XG1OV2P6uZZ5FSM9Ttw.

"Test Drive." Flutter.dev. Accessed July 2021. https://flutter.dev/docs/get-started/test-drive.

Other Resources

"Awesome Flutter Talks." GitHub. Accessed July 2021. https://github.com/Rahiche/awesome-flutter-talks.

Bizzotto, Andrea. "My Favoutire Lists of Flutter Resources." Medium, 2018 December 3. https://medium.com/coding-with-flutter/my-favourite-list-of-flutter-resources-523adc611cbe.

"Build a UI Login with Flutter." Pusher. Accessed July 2021. https://pusher.com/tutorials/login-ui-flutter.

"Dart Programming." TutorialsPoint. Accessed July 2021. https://www.tutorialspoint.com/dart_programming

"Flutter." GitHub. Accessed July 2021. https://github.com/flutter/flutter.

"Flutter: Introduction to Dart and Programming." Tutorials Point. Accessed July 2021. https://www.tutorialspoint.com/flutter/flutter_introduction_to_dart_programming.htm.

Gupta, Anmol. "Music Playing Using Flutter." Medium, 2021 August 8. https://medium.com/flutterdevs/music-player-using-flutter-a803c939c967.

Hiwarale, Uday. "Dart (DartLang) Introduction: Advanced Dart Features." Medium, 2019 October 7. https://medium.com/run-dart/dart-dartlang-introduction-advanced-dart-features-524de79456b9.

"How to Release Your Flutter App for iOS and Android." Instabug. Accessed July 2021. https://instabug.com/blog/how-to-release-your-flutter-app-for-ios-and-android.

Joshi, Devan. "The Complete Flutter Series: Exploring a Flutter Project and Building Your First Flutter App." Medium, 2018 June 28. https://medium.com/@dev.n/the-complete-flutter-series-article-1-exploring-a-flutter-project-and-building-your-first-flutter-e438ea941d70.

Khan, Sara. "Create Your App with Flutter in 5 Days." GitConnected, 31 March 2021. https://levelup.gitconnected.com/create-your-app-with-flutter-in-5-days-412ee41de22a.

Martin, Gonzalo. "Flutter: Creating an App from Scratch." Medium, 2018 July 2. https://medium.com/@gonzamartin87/flutter-creating-an-app-from-scratch-561d069579#8601

Srivastava, Naveen. "Debugging in Flutter." Medium, 2021 May 6. https://medium.com/flutterdevs/debugging-in-flutter-fb34832e31b0.

Suprastyo, Ecco. "Tutorial Ecommerce App Using Flutter." 2020 January 23. https://medium.com/@ekosuprastyo15/tutorial-ecommerce-app-using-flutter-96875d814c70

"What is Flutter? Benefits and Limitations." Code Magic, 2019 January 18. https://blog.codemagic.io/what-is-flutter-benefits-and-limitations.

Printed in Great Britain
by Amazon